JOSSEY-BASS TEACHER

Jossey-Bass Teacher provides K–12 teachers with essential knowledge and tools to create a positive and lifelong impact on student learning. Trusted and experienced educational mentors offer practical classroom-tested and theory-based teaching resources for improving teaching practice in a broad range of grade levels and subject areas. From one educator to another, we want to be your first source to make every day your best day in teaching. *Jossey-Bass Teacher* resources serve two types of informational needs—essential knowledge and essential tools.

Essential knowledge resources provide the foundation, strategies, and methods from which teachers may design curriculum and instruction to challenge and excite their students. Connecting theory to practice, essential knowledge books rely on a solid research base and time-tested methods, offering the best ideas and guidance from many of the most experienced and well-respected experts in the field.

Essential tools save teachers time and effort by offering proven, ready-to-use materials for in-class use. Our publications include activities, assessments, exercises, instruments, games, ready reference, and more. They enhance an entire course of study, a weekly lesson, or a daily plan. These essential tools provide insightful, practical, and comprehensive materials on topics that matter most to K–12 teachers.

Writing for a Change

Writing for a Change

BOOSTING LITERACY AND
LEARNING THROUGH
SOCIAL ACTION

Kristina Berdan, Ian Boulton,
Elyse Eidman-Aadahl, Jennie Fleming,
Launie Gardner, Iana Rogers,
and Asali Solomon
Editors

Foreword by Richard Sterling

JOSSEY-BASS
A Wiley Imprint
www.josseybass.com

Published by Jossey-Bass
A Wiley Imprint
989 Market Street, San Francisco, CA 94103-1741   www.josseybass.com

Jossey-Bass books and products are available through most bookstores. To contact Jossey-Bass directly call our Customer Care Department within the U.S. at 800-956-7739, outside the U.S. at 317-572-3986, or fax 317-572-4002.

Jossey-Bass also publishes its books in a variety of electronic formats. Some content that appears in print may not be available in electronic books.

Library of Congress Cataloging-in-Publication Data

Writing for a change: boosting literacy and learning through social action/
Kristina Berdan . . . [et al.] editors; foreword by Richard Sterling.
   p. cm.
 Includes bibliographical references and index.
 ISBN-13: 978-0-7879-8657-5 (alk. paper)
 ISBN-10: 0-7879-8657-7 (alk. paper)
 1. Language arts. 2. Written communication—Study and teaching.
3. English language—Composition and exercises—Study and teaching.
4. Social action. I. Berdan, Kristina.
LB1576.W735 2006
428.0071—dc22   2006022698

Printed in the United States of America
FIRST EDITION
PB Printing   10 9 8 7 6 5 4 3 2 1

CONTENTS

FOREWORD

I first learned about the Centre for Social Action from Mark Harrison—who is now working at the University of East Anglia in Norwich, England—while I was visiting Leicester, England, nearly twenty years ago. At the center of our discussion was a problem that has been on my mind almost the entire time that I have worked in education: Why do a significant number of young people simply leave school in both the United Kingdom and the United States, reporting that they found school boring, uninteresting, alienating? When I began teaching first-generation college students at the City University of New York, I was regaled with stories about how grim these students' school experiences had been for them. Their stories mirrored my own high school experience in the United Kingdom, so the center's work with young people in out-of-school settings captured my attention personally and professionally.

Mark Harrison, who was at that time the director of the Centre for Social Action at De Montfort University in Leicester, England, convinced me that the center's success in various communities was no accident. Elyse Eidman-Aadahl and I went to see for ourselves. What we saw in after-school and community centers was indeed impressive. We met a range of people from the center, such as Professor Dave Ward, Jennie Fleming, and Ian Boulton, who were building a tradition of work with youths that had no direct parallel here in the United States. Our task at the National Writing Project was to introduce this work into the U.S. context, make adaptations where necessary, and see whether the lines between in-school work and after-school work might be blurred so that students would continue to gain academic strength while engaging in the Social Action process, which was exciting and rewarding. This book is the story of those efforts. Program director Elyse Eidman-Aadahl, along with staff members Iana Rogers and Asali Solomon, provided the leadership and infrastructure that made this work possible, along with Jennie Fleming and Ian Boulton from the Centre for Social Action. Then the participating teachers, whose stories are reported here, worked to make the practices their own.

Young people in our society need to be engaged in learning, in designing projects that are bigger than themselves, and in doing work that brings them into frequent contact with caring adults. The good news is that, as the teachers in this volume demonstrate, this can be done. We have much to learn from these teachers and the young people with whom they work.

Berkeley, California
July 2006

Richard Sterling
Executive Director
National Writing Project

NW**P**

The National Writing Project (NWP) is a nationwide professional development program for teachers, begun in 1974 at the University of California, Berkeley. Organized as a network of close to two hundred university-based writing project sites in all fifty states, Washington, D.C., Puerto Rico, and the U.S. Virgin Islands, the NWP is dedicated to improving student writing and learning in the nation's schools by supporting high-quality professional development for K–16 teachers. Collectively, these sites serve approximately 100,000 educators every year, grades kindergarten through university, in all disciplines. The NWP views quality education as a cornerstone of equity and democracy. Its model is based on the belief that teachers are key to education reform, that teachers can be leaders in professional learning communities, and that teachers benefit from lifelong learning communities in which they can study theory and research and can conduct inquiry into their own practice. For more information on the National Writing Project or to find a site near you, visit www.writingproject.org.

The Centre for Social Action is a training, consulting, research, and publications unit based at De Montfort University in Leicester, England. The center works alongside practitioners, managers, and community members in a range of settings, including social work, health, youth work, housing, and regeneration (redevelopment), with the aim of achieving positive social change through community development, project development, and professional development. The center promotes Social Action, an approach that enables groups of people of all ages and circumstances to take action to achieve their collectively identified goals. Involvement with the center is open to anyone with an interest in the Social Action approach. For more information, visit www.dmu.ac.uk/dmucsa.

Young people have an extraordinary capacity to pursue learning that engages them—*outside* of school. Surrounded by and marketed an attractive set of options, from the media to the Internet to the friendship group, young people find ways to pursue issues that matter to them with tremendous energy. *Inside* of schools, though, teachers struggle to harness that energy for the purposes, knowledge, and skills that schooling is supposed to foster. Recent educational policy has focused on articulating and systematizing those purposes, knowledge, and skills while raising the stakes of their mastery for both teachers and students. Teachers may be experiencing something like Dewey's classic contradiction of the child versus the curriculum (Dewey, 1956). Do we attend to the interests of the students, perhaps fostering engagement at the expense of covering the standards and curriculum? Or do we push on through the expanding curriculum and battery of tests, perhaps sacrificing student engagement or choice? And what if the central focus of your curriculum—for example, the teaching of writing— can only be fully addressed when the child is really engaged with the task at hand? Writing about the tendency to see attention to the child and his needs as in conflict with attention to curriculum, Dewey argued, "Any significant problem involves conditions that for the moment contradict each other. Solution comes only by . . . coming to see the conditions from another point of view, and hence in a fresh light" (Dewey, 1956, pp. 3–4).

SHINING A FRESH LIGHT

Harnessing students' enormous energy, facilitating their engagement in learning, and managing high-stakes curricular pressures are some of the issues that led teachers and leaders affiliated with the National Writing Project (NWP) to begin a multiyear collaboration with practitioners engaged in youth work at the Centre for Social Action (CSA), based in England. For over twenty years, the CSA has been developing principles and practices for youth-driven action by working with young people in a range of settings outside of school. Experienced at working with young people in community settings where they can easily vote with their feet, the center's practitioners emphasize engaging and facilitating groups of young people in work that matters to them because it addresses and acts on the content of their lives and communities. Drawing on intellectual antecedents like Paulo Freire, these practitioners have refined an approach to group and community work they call *Social Action*. In the Social Action approach, youth workers support young people in sharing and examining issues that affect them in their daily lives, then learning skills and implementing plans to take productive action in their lives and communities.

In 2001, a team of educators at the National Writing Project, a U.S.-based teacher network with a thirty-year history of improving the teaching of writing, became intrigued by the Social Action approach and wondered whether it could shine a fresh light on the contradictions they were experiencing as teachers. As literacy educators, they too expected young people to engage in projects that mattered to them and to learn and use complex literacy skills to act in their lives and communities. They knew that in learning any set of skills, whether personal, athletic, or academic, engagement mattered. Young people cannot learn what they won't engage with. Social Action workers had figured out how to get the most marginalized young people engaged in complex and demanding work outside of school. NWP teachers interested in a more student-driven learning environment wondered, Could CSA approaches work with American young people *inside* of school, with its prescribed curriculum and compulsory demands? Practitioners at the Centre for Social Action wondered too.

Thus began an inquiry into the potential for the Social Action work inside schools. Through a four-year collaboration, NWP teachers and CSA trainers worked together to see how teachers would make sense of Social Action ideas in their practice. Although the center's experiences and ways of working initially seemed distant from the realities of U.S. schools, teachers from the National Writing Project soon identified important insights for their work and began exploring new opportunities for student-driven learning and literacy in their schools and curriculum. Together, they found that Social Action had tremendous potential for engaging students and creating a context for boosting literacy and achievement in schools. Working through processes facilitated by a leadership and editorial team, participating teachers refined those lessons with a view toward sharing their experiences with their colleagues.

In this book, some of the teachers and trainers who took part in the NWP-CSA collaboration share their successes, challenges, and continuing questions about using Social Action in their teaching. Following their accounts, workers from the Centre for Social Action describe the theory and principles that form the foundation of the Social Action approach and share some of the activities and resources used during the cross-national workshops, including a wide set of activities to get groups of people involved with Social Action.

OVERVIEW OF THE BOOK

A history of the NWP-CSA collaboration and an overview of key questions that informed the work is presented in Chapter One. In Part One, nine teachers and many students describe their experiences with Social Action in the classroom and the community. In some cases, teachers and students describe full efforts to use Social Action and learn about its implications. In other cases, teachers describe how specific practices or principles of Social Action led them to reevaluate and sometimes change aspects of their teaching or curriculum. Chapters Two through Six illustrate the flexibility of Social Action in school settings. In Chapter Two, Paula Laub shows how she wove Social Action into the fabric of her first-grade classroom as she describes her journey from sole problem solver to one of twenty problem solvers in her classroom. In Chapter Three, Dietta Hitchcock shares how

Social Action led her to design a new curriculum, with her students' help. Student members of Youth Dreamers write about the long, difficult process of creating a youth-run youth center in Chapter Four, while their teacher, Kristina Berdan, reflects on the role of Social Action in their work and in her English and language arts classroom in Chapter Five. In Chapter Six, Chinwe Obijiofor describes how she used the Social Action process in a summer program while also portraying the tension between engaging young people in social or political activism as understood by adults and the youth-driven process of Social Action.

Chapters Seven through Ten share the reflections of teachers and students who took on particular aspects of Social Action as a way to expand and rethink student involvement in curriculum and in the social life of schools. In Chapter Seven, Lori Farias and her students highlight how Social Action helped students take greater control of their choices in service learning, a requirement of her high school English elective course. In Chapter Eight, Maggie Folkers, another high school teacher, shares how she used Social Action activities at the start of her semester to create a community of learners, who then used these activities when participating in critical reflection throughout the course. Connie Bunch, in Chapter Nine, writes about how she used Social Action to help students find ways to defuse explosive situations among peers. And in Chapter Ten, Elizabeth Davis shares how what started as a lesson on the civil rights movement turned into an opportunity for her middle school students to save their school. Concluding Part One, Chapter Eleven presents a window into Social Action work with adults through the story of how Mildred Serra collaborated with parents from a marginalized community near her school in Puerto Rico. In Serra's chapter, we see that these parents not only attended a series of Social Action workshops but also took their experiences from these workshops and continued to better their community long after the workshops were over.

These examples of practice, which come from teachers working in a range of public schools, urban and rural, illustrate the flexibility and adaptability of Social Action to a wide range of purposes and settings. In Part Two, the editors look back at this diversity of examples and tie it to the theory, processes, and principles developed by the CSA over time. Chapter Twelve synthesizes what NWP teachers found to be the tensions between Social Action practice and traditional teaching practice and explores both the challenges and benefits of integrating Social Action in the classroom. In Chapter Thirteen Jennie Fleming, director of the Centre for Social Action at De Montfort University in Leicester, and Ian Boulton, director of the Social Action Company and a former trainer at the Centre for Social Action, present the theory and practice of Social Action as developed at the center. Finally, in Chapter Fourteen, Fleming and Boulton present a series of questions and issues for consideration by teachers who are interested in exploring Social Action in their own teaching. Readers who wish to explore the theory first should begin with Part Two.

For teachers who are interested in taking some steps with Social Action, Part Three offers practical advice and activities for beginning Social Action work in various settings. Part Three provides detailed descriptions of activities that were used in cross-national training sessions or created by practitioners. This is followed by References and then by Resources for Further Reading, which were selected to help you get started on your own journeys with Social Action. Together, these closing sections aim to support the idea that there is nothing so practical as a good theory—and that practitioners working together within a theoretical tradition, in praxis, can sharpen and develop its insights.

Now, from the vantage point of our four-year collaboration, we can say that Dewey was right, that even at a time when we feel caught between the energies of youth and the escalating demands of curriculum, there are ways out of the contradiction. The teacher-facilitators whose essays are collected in this volume would not say that learning and applying the Social Action approach has always been easy; as Dewey slyly observed, recasting contradictions "means travail of thought" (Dewey, 1956, p. 4). The pressures and contradictions of teaching in the current policy environment cannot be wished away. But we don't have to choose between our students and our curriculum. The Social Action approach is not about simply giving young people what they want or giving up on learning at the highest levels. It is a disciplined and focused process of engagement in collective action. Together, we saw that our students—many of whom were not engaged in traditional school activities—engaged with the Social Action process because it was based on their interests and concerns and because they directed what was happening. A sense of control, for both students and for teachers, creates powerful conditions for learning. Despite the unconventional approach, the carefully managed process of Social Action could result in traditional learning being valued by students in school and in college—not the child versus the curriculum but the child *and* the curriculum.

Kristina Berdan has been a teacher for eight years and currently teaches language arts to seventh graders at the Stadium School in Baltimore, Maryland. She also works with sixth-, seventh-, and eighth-grade Youth Dreamers at school and is president of the Stadium School Youth Dreamers, Inc., working alongside youth officers. A National Board Certified Teacher, she is also a part-time faculty member at Towson University and a teacher-consultant with the Maryland Writing Project.

Ian Boulton has worked as a trainer and community worker for twenty-five years. He is a partner in The Social Action Company, a group of consultants that use Social Action methods to develop social care and community projects in Eastern Europe.

Connie Ellard Bunch, a teacher-consultant with the Alcorn Writing Project in Natchez, Mississippi, has taught for fifteen years. Her experience includes teaching English as a second language in Japan and in adult education, public schools, and private schools in Kentucky, Mississippi, and Louisiana. She is certified in gifted education, special education, and elementary education and holds National Board Certification in Adolescence and Young Adulthood/English Language Arts.

Critics of Society is a one-semester, untracked English class consisting of juniors and seniors at Sparks High School in Sparks, Nevada. The class of 2003 co-wrote the piece "Changing Our World."

Elizabeth A. Davis is a teacher-consultant with the D.C. Area Writing Project and a veteran technology education teacher in the District of Columbia Public Schools. In addition to serving on the Urban Sites Network leadership team of the National

Writing Project, Elizabeth currently teaches at John Philip Sousa Middle School in Southeast Washington, D.C.

Elyse Eidman-Aadahl directs national programs and site development for the National Writing Project (NWP) at the University of California, Berkeley. A former high school English teacher and university teacher educator, she has been both a teacher-participant and a national leader in a range of teacher learning networks in the NWP and in other professional organizations. Her founding work with the collaboration between the NWP and the Centre for Social Action grows out of a long-standing interest in teachers' learning from literacy work and youth work in out-of-school settings.

Lori Farias is a teacher-consultant with the Northern Nevada Writing Project at the University of Nevada, Reno. She has been teaching for over a decade and currently teaches eleventh and twelfth graders as a language arts teacher at Sparks High School in Sparks, Nevada.

Jennie Fleming began her working life as a youth and community worker on voluntary and statutory youth work projects in the United Kingdom. Since 1995, she has worked actively to develop Social Action practice at the Centre for Social Action (CSA) at De Montfort University in England. She has been part of the collaboration between the CSA and the National Writing Project from its inception.

Maggie Folkers has been an educator for fourteen years and currently teaches World Cultures, a team-taught honors class of sixty sophomores, and two junior-senior classes of Poetry and Mythology at Edward C. Reed High School in Sparks, Nevada, where she chairs the English department. She has been an active teacher-consultant for the Northern Nevada Writing Project since 2001.

Launie Gardner has been a teacher for sixteen years and currently teaches eleventh- and twelfth-grade English, civics, and economics at Truckee Meadows Community College High School in Reno, Nevada. She also serves as co-chair of the board of directors of Rainshadow Community Charter High School, a school that is attempting to integrate interdisciplinary, project-based, and community-based hands-on learning. She served as director for the Northern Nevada Writing Project and remains involved with its professional development activities focused on Social Action.

Dietta Poston Hitchcock has taught gifted education in elementary and junior high schools for six years. Currently, she is teaching art to students in kindergarten through fifth grade in six schools and helping to develop curriculum for the new arts program in the Roswell school district in New Mexico. She is a teacher-consultant with the High Plains Writing Project.

Paula Laub has been a teacher for eight years. She currently teaches second grade at Paradise Professional Development School in Las Vegas, Nevada. Paula is also a teacher-consultant for the Southern Nevada Writing Project at the University of Nevada, Las Vegas, and is an active member of the Social Action committee for their site.

Chinwe "La Tanya" Obijiofor, a reading specialist at Wynbrooke Elementary School in Stone Mountain, Georgia, is a veteran teacher of twenty years and holds National Board Certification as an Early Childhood/Generalist. In addition to her duties as a teacher, she works with the Georgia Professional Standards Commission as one of the Reach-to-Teach faculty members. She has served as director of the Peachtree Urban Writing Project's Summer Writing Institute for Students in Atlanta, Georgia.

Iana Rogers is national programs manager for the National Writing Project (NWP) at the University of California, Berkeley. She has been working with the collaboration between the NWP and the Centre for Social Action since 2001.

Mildred Serra has been a teacher for twenty-four years in private and public schools in Puerto Rico and is currently an English teacher for fourth and fifth grades at Lorencita Ramirez de Arellano School in Toa Baja, Puerto Rico. She is a teacher-consultant with the Borinquen Writing Project at the University of Sacred Heart in Santurce, Puerto Rico.

Asali Solomon has been working with the National Writing Project collaboration with the Centre for Social Action since 2000. She is currently assistant professor of English at Washington & Lee University in Lexington, Virginia, where she teaches African American literature, composition, and creative writing and often uses Social Action activities with her students.

The Youth Dreamers (Mildred Harris, Chantel Morant, Shanta Crippen, Chris Lawson, Chekana Reid, Cierra Cary, and Tiffani Young-Smith) are a group of students in grades six through eleven who decided in 2001 to create a youth-run youth center in their community in Baltimore, Maryland, to give young people like themselves a positive place to go after school. These authors come from different generations of Youth Dreamers; some have stayed committed to the project past their years at the Stadium School where the project began, and some are just beginning to work in the classroom at the Stadium School.

Writing for a Change

Exploring Student-Driven Learning and Literacy Through Social Action

For decades, literacy educators have explored the complicated practices that invite and respond to student interest and social purpose. Some things, they argue, can only be learned when a writer is engaged with a real rhetorical situation, with something important to accomplish and something of her own to say. In those magical moments of engagement, the writer feels a need to learn what the teacher is eager to teach. Teachers working within the traditions of what John Willinsky has called "the New Literacy" (Willinsky, 1990) actively pursue occasions when they can position themselves side by side with student writers, coaching them through complex decisions about stance and substance, using the community of writers as a resource, teaching essential skills at the point of need, and responding to the work, confident that the writers' commitment to the larger project will carry them through to the next draft. Sometimes, in classrooms of writers, those occasions attain a sense of collective purpose, and literacy learning is experienced as a social and political practice that is potentially transformative.

But in the next breath, teachers note that such occasions seem all too rare, that creating an engaged community of shared purpose within the confines of the public school classroom is challenging, and that taking students' real interests and purposes seriously raises a host of very real professional and curricular dilemmas. Add to these internal challenges an often unstable school reform environment and high-stakes assessment and accountability programs that can discourage innovation by teachers and students alike, and we might not be surprised to see educators turn their attention to other professional concerns. Yet the vision *is* compelling.

COLLABORATING ON THE VISION

The ongoing interest of literacy educators in the potential of student-driven curriculum work is the foundation for the work reported in this book. *Writing for a Change: Boosting Literacy and Learning Through Social Action* presents a sampler of work by U.S. teachers that grew out of an ongoing collaboration between teachers in the National Writing Project (NWP) and practitioners from the Centre for Social Action (CSA) in the United Kingdom. Sparked by personal connections between the directors of the two organizations, the partnership between the NWP and the CSA eventuated in a cross-national exchange among practitioners seeking more positive ways to engage with marginalized young people and to support the learning of adults who work with them.

As collaborators, the two organizations brought together very different centers of expertise. The Centre for Social Action has been articulating and refining a progressive approach to professional practice in community work, youth work, and social work for more than twenty years. Working in a variety of out-of-school settings, first locally in the United Kingdom, then internationally, Social Action practitioners have trained groups to use Social Action methods to work together to improve conditions in their local communities. Social Action was developed by practitioners working in youth and community work in England. By looking to service users as the drivers of community change and framing service providers as supporters and facilitators, they created a body of work that offers both a set of principles and a methodology that can be used by facilitators working with groups pursuing change.

The National Writing Project, a network of nearly two hundred university-based local writing projects, has worked for over thirty years to build a professional culture in which teachers work together to learn, conduct research, and improve the teaching of writing. The NWP has created methods and approaches that are carefully fitted to the occupational culture and potential of teaching as a profession.

Serving roughly 100,000 teachers a year, the NWP approach to reform looks to the leadership of its cadre of teacher-consultants—local educators who staff and manage writing project sites and programs. When a group of these teacher-consultants was introduced to the Social Action approach through the National Writing Project, they were simultaneously intrigued and skeptical. Would an approach developed in the comparably open settings of community centers and youth organizations translate to the formal and tightly managed settings of public schools? Would professional practices originally employed in the helping professions translate to teaching, where delivery of prescribed content and skills has come to define professional practice? How would Social Action work fit within a teacher's responsibility to his faculty, to larger curricular programs, or to extant school reform models? Nonetheless, despite their initial questions, teachers believed the partnership would introduce them to methods and practices that would challenge and therefore strengthen their approaches to student-driven curriculum practices. They recommended going forward with a collaboration.

The NWP-CSA collaboration began by supporting cross-visitation of practitioners: classroom teachers from the NWP and youth workers from the CSA. Beginning in 2001, the NWP; the Bay Area Writing Project at the University of California, Berkeley; and the New York City Writing Project hosted visits of CSA affiliated leaders and youth workers, who toured classrooms and youth development programs. The following year, NWP program director Elyse Eidman-Aadahl and a group of five NWP teachers attended a Social Action Summer Institute program in Chester, England. The success of both visits, and the confirmation that practitioners inside and outside of schools did indeed have much to share, led the two organizations to experiment with a series of training sessions for NWP teachers across the country. Led by Social Action facilitators Jennie Fleming and Ian Boulton, these workshops focused on Social Action as a process and invited teachers to consider its application in their classrooms as well as in the community and organizational settings Fleming and Boulton had worked in. A network of teachers from these workshops soon began experimenting with Social Action in their classrooms and leading study groups at their local writing project sites. Their explorations were as varied as their urban and rural public school settings. Maryland Writing Project teacher-consultant Kristina Berdan, for example, began working with her students to form a group called the Youth Dreamers. Five years later, this group of public school students in Baltimore is well on the way to opening their own youth-run youth center—a dramatic story that links in-school work with out-of-school community engagement. Many other teachers also began experimenting with Social Action approaches as they reworked common classroom procedures or bits of curriculum. While their work may be less publicly visible, it suggests that Social Action can be worked into the basic fabric of schooling in a way that invites greater student engagement, responsibility, and control in the school community. Their work points to an equally powerful sense of possibility: the possibility of looking to youth as leaders and managers within the routines of daily life in school.

Over the several years following the initial training workshops, the collaboration gained momentum through continuing institutes and cross-visitation. The network of teachers met in the summer to probe experiences, look for patterns, and challenge each other's assumptions. Teachers have shared experiences at the NWP's annual and network meetings, and teacher-consultants from such diverse sites as Nevada; the Washington, D.C., metropolitan area; and Alcorn State Writing Project in Natchez, Mississippi, have presented their work and introduced others to Social Action. In 2002, these presentations culminated at an event at the NWP Annual Meeting titled "Doing Social Action in the Writing Project," which included teacher-consultants from Borinquen Writing Project in Puerto Rico; High Plains Writing Project in New Mexico; Peachtree Urban Writing Project in Atlanta; Philadelphia Writing Project; and Acadiana Writing Project in Louisiana. The stories and experiences shared through these forums are the foundation of this book.

SOCIAL ACTION IN THE NATIONAL WRITING PROJECT

Social Action practice in the NWP embodies ideas that are not new to literacy educators: faith in student potential, the idea that each student is a valuable contributor, the sense that real substance and complex tasks matter in the classroom, the importance of looking openly at one's professional identity, and the sense that each of us, teacher and student, has to take ownership of her own learning. As writing teachers, many participating teachers understood Social Action as a larger structure for engaging students in action projects that would require and motivate the kinds of complex uses of reading and writing that are necessary for later success in college and in life. Teachers saw avenues for student-driven research, for writing as a tool for community building and joint planning, for involving students in public presentations and extensive reflection. Again, this felt familiar.

However, as many participating teachers had hoped, Social Action did push them to the unfamiliar as well. Social Action is a process whereby young people consider *what* issues and problems concern them, analyze *why* they exist, consider *how* they can act to change them, take these *actions,* and then *reflect* on what they have done and what has changed. Facilitated as a group process, the work is informed by the principles of Social Action: a commitment to work for social justice; the belief that all people have the right to be heard, to define the issues that are facing them, and to take action on their own behalf; and the expectation that all people have skills, knowledge, and experience they can use to address problems they face.

These principles resonated with most of the teachers, but acting on them in the context of schools proved complex. Furthermore, many teachers came to the work from schools serving young people from marginalized communities and drew on a history of work in social justice. Social Action recognizes that oppression and injustice are complex issues rooted in social and economic practices and policy— again, a perspective that resonated with teachers. Social Action believes that while people may experience the impact of oppression and injustice individually, these issues must be recognized and addressed as social problems by facilitating processes whereby people collectively learn to discover the parts of their lives that they can change. Social Action addresses commitment to justice through a process where adults or professionals are not to act as experts but as facilitators in a social change process. This approach requires self-discipline from all adults, even the most polit- ically aware, to make sure that the agenda, issues, and analysis really come from the young people. Teachers discovered that even the most youth-supportive among them were challenged when young people's perspectives on their lives diverged from adults' agendas.

Ultimately, exploring an approach that had been developed outside of the taken-for-granted assumptions of schooling and of teachers' and students' roles led participating teachers to rigorously reexamine their role in the classroom com- munity and their relationship with their students across many dimensions, often surfacing contradictions in their practice. Teachers who generally acknowledged their students' ideas in writing wondered whether they had constructed them- selves into different and contradictory roles elsewhere in the classroom. Other teachers were pushed to consider strategies and practices for joint action with col- leagues or with parents. Engaging with CSA workers who typically worked in actual communities motivated them to explore the boundaries of the metaphor of classroom community. Some were pushed to rethink the design of their courses or of the opportunities for culminating tasks and projects. Across these differences, teachers saw themselves as setting aside the notion that teachers make classrooms *for* their students in favor of the notion that students and teachers construct classrooms *together*.

As a result, the work reported in this book focuses less on the traditional concerns of teachers of writing and more on exploring new applications for Social Action in classrooms and curriculums. Teachers have integrated aspects of Social Action into diverse areas, using it in basic literacy classes and after-school clubs, for environmental justice projects and for working with young people affected by poverty. The pieces that follow illustrate teachers using the steps of the Social Action process to build communities in classrooms at all levels, first grade through high school, and to make significant connections between schools and community members that had previously been isolated from each other. Social Action has provided a structure for diverse endeavors, from a community project for parents in San Juan, Puerto Rico, to the efforts of first graders to change school library policy and expedite the building of a playground.

Despite the common ground between writing project practice and the Social Action approach, working with Social Action methods within the expectations of traditional schooling and the demands of the teacher's role has been challenging as well as rewarding. As Jennie Fleming and Ian Boulton explain in Chapter Thirteen, Social Action workers responsible for a group project are facilitators rather than leaders. This calls for Social Action workers to share authority at the deepest levels, including the authority to name and negotiate the content and scope of the work, as well as its aims and goals. With service users in the lead in determining the nature and aims of their joint work, facilitators play a key role in helping the group learn how to direct and learn from their efforts. Facilitators and community members form, in essence, a community development partnership.

Teachers, of course, are responsible for education and discipline in their classrooms and are expected to be authorities on the content of the curriculum as well as on standards and assessment. Professionally and legally accountable to their school system and, ultimately, to parents and the public, teachers are positioned to represent a certain sort of social authority that could be seen as being at odds with the role of facilitator. Indeed in the United States, the notion of the teacher as a facilitator has sometimes been associated with an anti-intellectual and content-free concept of teaching that is seemingly distant from concerns with academic achievement. Teachers working with Social Action struggled with the nature and role of teacher authority in their classrooms and considered deeply how to responsibly share that authority while promoting achievement.

As a central part of Social Action practice, workers create and facilitate groups so that work for change is collective, the struggle of a community. Participating teachers, who valued new ways to actualize their classroom as a community, were nonetheless challenged to think through the balance of group and individual needs, interests, and capacities. For some teachers, thinking about the notion of group formation and facilitation and their implications for classroom communities became as strong an interest as the Social Action process. This interest gave new life to practices that depend on the classroom community as a resource for learning. Still, in their professional role, teachers are accountable for ensuring that all students attain particular skills and capacities as individuals within the group, and they must learn how to manage group work when the ongoing assignment and the presence of members is compulsory rather than voluntary.

A final and specific tension for participating teachers was the tension between the Social Action approach and the central commitment of the National Writing Project to the importance of writing. Social Action was developed by youth workers as a way of engaging young people who were marginalized from school. Many had left school and had negative associations with writing and literacy. Although the CSA works with a variety of professionals as well as young people, the practice remains one that is not dependent on a participant's literacy skills. Therefore, a majority of the Social Action activities that trainers shared with NWP teachers required minimal writing, depending instead on other means of participating: speaking, drawing, creative dramatics, and so on. Not willing to set aside the potential of literacy, NWP teacher-consultants created a Social Action practice that includes writing and teaches literacy along with other types of communication. Indeed, the use of writing at all stages of the process is key to accomplishing the academic goals they are responsible for. NWP teachers developed activities that used writing for individual and group exploration and reflection, for planning and management of group action, and often as the substance of action itself. Students were introduced to ways that their literacy skills could be used to accomplish purposes they valued in the world, and in the process, they became committed to improving those skills. The teachers have made Social Action their own by using Social Action to improve literacy.

And of course, they have made it their own by writing about their experiences with Social Action. We invite you to make it your own, too.

PART ONE

Social Action in Practice

In this section, NWP teachers who have used Social Action in their work share their stories. Located in a wide variety of contexts, urban and rural, and involving young people of all ages, their experiences illustrate the flexibility and adaptability of Social Action principles and processes both in the classroom and, in one case, in working with parents in a community-based setting. Some of these teacher-facilitators have given over their classroom entirely to the principles and process of Social Action, while others have used elements of it to develop their work with young people—perhaps by seizing on serendipitous "teachable moments."

Despite the diversity, the teachers' experiences have many core elements in common. All of these teachers choose to adopt the role of teacher-facilitator in a way that is informed by the processes of Social Action. In these examples, they invite young people (and, in one case, community members) to consider *what* issues and problems concern them, analyze *why* they exist, consider *how* they can take action to change them, take these *actions*, and then *reflect* on what they have done and what has changed. All are also clearly informed by the principles of Social Action: a commitment to work for social justice; a recognition that all people have skills, knowledge, and experience that they can use to address problems they face; and a belief that all people have the right to be heard, to define the issues that are facing them, and to take action on their own behalf. Social Action also recognizes that oppression and injustice are complex issues rooted in social and economic practices and policy; while people may experience the impact of oppression and injustice individually, these issues must be recognized and addressed as social problems. In addition, these stories highlight the motivational aspects of Social Action. The young people, many of whom did not typically engage in school activities, pursued Social Action enthusiastically because they directed what was happening. Finally, all the examples illustrate that despite its unconventional approach, Social Action can result in the academic achievement that we all value.

Power Play

PAULA LAUB

"It's not fair, Mrs. Laub!" After seven years of teaching, I had heard those five words many times. However, when these words were uttered on one particular day, I had no idea that they would be the impetus for a journey on which I was about to embark—an experience that would forever alter my beliefs about student voice in my classroom.

It was a typical day in my urban first-grade classroom in Las Vegas, Nevada. My nineteen students, a majority of them from low-income homes in which a language other than English was spoken, were just returning from the library. Everything seemed normal as they gathered on the carpeted meeting area to listen to a story. As I began reading, I could sense that all was not right with their world. So I asked them, "Is there something we need to talk about?" Nothing. All I saw were heads turning and eyes darting from one face to another. I spoke again: "I can't fix it if I don't know what's wrong." Finally, someone spoke. One of my students who spoke English, but not without putting a lot of thought and effort into what he was saying, spoke up.

"She wouldn't let us check out any books we wanted to!" he said.

"Who?" I asked.

"The librarian said we had to check out books with those dots."

The colored dots to which Edgar was referring were placed on the books to match students with particular reading levels. Each color is assigned a reading level, and students are to check out books in "their" reading range. My students were aware of this practice, but in Reader's Workshop, which is the program we do in our classroom, students read books of their choice.

Edgar, who seemed to have taken the role of speaker for the whole class, continued with his complaint: "This is our library too, and when I go to the other library [the public library], I can get any books I want!" This seemed to be the cue for other students to chime in. The comments came slowly at first. Then everyone had something to say.

"I can take books home that are too hard for me and have someone read it to me."

"We know you can read by looking at the pictures."

"How come if the library is for everyone, only certain books are for us?"

I couldn't believe how angry and impatient I was becoming. My first instinct was to march right down to the librarian and explain to her why this was so unfair not only to my students but to all students at our school. Then I thought that maybe I should just take it directly to the principal. After all, she knew how I ran my classroom. I have always taught my children about the importance of making good choices and have tried to provide ample opportunities for them to practice making choices in our classroom community. Surely she would listen to me, and then this book access problem would be settled. I am such an enlightened teacher, I thought. Or am I? Wait. I am such a hypocritical teacher.

The "shoulds" and "coulds" of this situation resonated in my mind in the course of about a minute. Then reality hit again: I am a hypocritical teacher. Perhaps I am being a little hard on myself, but at that moment, I remembered what I had just said: "I can't fix it if I don't know what's wrong." I had just communicated to my students that the only power and voice they had was confined within the four walls of our classroom. Anything that happened outside of Room Five was beyond their control. I asked myself what had caused me to automatically react that way when they presented their problem to me. Did I not trust them? Did I not believe that they had the power to change things that they felt were unfair? Did I view myself as *the* one to make change in our classroom and beyond? Why did I have to be the one to fix the problem? "Trust the process" is what Social Action promotes, right?

As I glanced into nineteen pairs of trusting eyes, I saw it—opportunity. I saw power in numbers. I saw a group with a common goal. I saw voices to make change. But this time was different. It wasn't my voice that was going to be heard. It was theirs.

As a novice to the Social Action process, I wasn't sure what the next step should be. I knew that the students had decided what the problem was. Why this was a problem had been voiced during the class discussion that followed identification of the problem. Because the discussion was happening so rapidly, I didn't have the opportunity to stop and think about which step was next in the Social Action process. Instead, I listened to the children and proceeded to facilitate them through what I thought was the next logical step.

How were they going to solve this problem? When I posed this question to them, it was obvious that many of them assumed that their inability to check out the books they wanted was my problem, not theirs. My question was answered with blank stares. I fought my natural urge to assure them that I would take care of this problem. I restated my question, but this time, I asked, "If this is something so important to you and you think it's unfair, how are you going to change it so that it is fair?" At this point, I still wasn't certain whether my students were taking me seriously. I think some were still thinking or maybe even hoping I was going to find a solution to the problem. I would tell them how to fix it, and they would just do it. I didn't. "Well?" I asked them again. A tiny voice from the back spoke up: "What if we told her [the librarian] why we don't like this rule?" asked Lucia. "Okay, how would you do that?" I questioned. "We could tell her at lunch," Alexa replied. "You sure could, and just remember what you said earlier about why you don't think this procedure is fair."

After about ten minutes, we had three different ideas for a solution: talk to the librarian in person, write the librarian a letter telling her why this practice of book checkout wasn't fair, or stop going to the library. Although I wasn't a fan of the last choice, I listed it as an option. At this point, I wasn't sure what to do. Did everyone get to choose from the ideas presented? Should I tell them that the third idea really isn't a viable solution? I asked each child to decide on one of the ways they were going to act. I'm not sure whether that was what I was supposed to do, but that is what I did. No one that I'm aware of spoke to the librarian at lunch, and no one wanted to stop going to the library. Several of the students did decide to write letters to the librarian explaining to her why they thought the book checkout process was unfair.

After school that day, I took the letters to our librarian, Mrs. Patterson. She is an older librarian, and I feared she might view the letters as disrespectful, but her reaction was quite the opposite. She was very impressed by the way my students were able to explain their concerns. Even if their explanations were marked by misspellings and lacked many conventions, their messages were loud and clear: not being able to check out books of their choice was so unfair. Their voices were heard, and their reason honored. My class was allowed to check out the books of their choice from that point on.

Fast-forward a year. Same room, same school, same population of students, and the same questions remained about how to create a safe and open classroom environment. How could I continue using literacy as my avenue to ensure that problem solving and change are a natural part of the classroom climate? I envisioned the first six weeks of school as a critical time, just like I always do. I wanted to integrate more of the students' voices right from the start. I wanted to allow them opportunities to have a voice in classroom decisions.

We began the year by developing our classroom rules. This year, however, the word *rules* was replaced by the word *promises*. These were our promises to each other as a developing community of learners. Using the word *promises* seemed like a minor detail at the time, but it gave my students a sense of ownership because it indicated that these were ideas that they had developed and agreed on rather than a set of imposed rules with predetermined consequences formulated by me. It's amazing how much respect and attention my students gave to these statements. Each member of our community was expected to keep these promises and agreed to this by printing their name on a written copy of them.

We also had weekly class meetings in which we could discuss our accomplishments as a class and as individuals. It was also an opportunity to address any issues we might be facing. These meetings always began with me reading from a book. I usually read a story that addressed an issue I had seen occurring in our classroom. Perhaps the story would encourage a discussion or evoke the need to write and reflect. During one of our classroom meetings, I again found myself face to face with opportunity.

I had begun to dread picking up my students from lunch. It seemed like every day there was some major catastrophe that had occurred the instant the bell rang to signal the end of lunch recess. Tattletales ran rampant. On one particular day, I was greeted with so many tattles and stories of pushing and shoving that I had just about had it! I conveniently became hard of hearing during our short walk from the blacktop to our room. The students entered the room quietly, because they could tell I was not in the best of moods by this time. After they sat down on the floor in the meeting area, I voiced my disgust with the behaviors I was hearing about every day after lunch. "Something had better change—and change now," I said. That was the end of this one-sided conversation. Problem solved. In my mind, the change I had envisioned was in the students' behaviors.

I quickly racked my brain for a nice picture book to calm them—and me—down. I happened to grab the book *A Fine, Fine School,* by Sharon Creech. I began to read this story about a school that was so wonderful that no one ever wanted to leave it. Throughout the story, I modeled think-alouds, sharing the connections I was making while reading the story. Normally, I am not able to get a word in edge-wise as my students command the floor with their thoughts and their personal connections. On that day, this was not the case. Perhaps they were all just so disappointed in their own behavior outside. Or perhaps I was oblivious to what they were really thinking.

By the end of the book, I was quite curious about why this story didn't elicit the conversation I was hoping for, so I asked my students whether they thought our school was like the school in the story. What were things we liked about our school? There were a few responses to that question, but nothing extraordinary: "We like P.E." "I like to read and write." Okay. So I went to the other end of the spectrum and asked them whether there was anything at our school that we didn't like. That must have been the opening my students had been waiting for. The floodgate had been opened! What was amazing to me, though, was how the conversation unfolded. This was still pretty early in the year, and normally, we practice for months and months how to listen intently to others, how to wait our turn, and how to have a discussion without needing to raise hands.

The students were pretty patient and respectful of each other as, one by one, they vocalized their complaints about our school. In a nutshell, the main problem was "We don't have a playground to play on anymore." Because we are a year-round school, there is not an opportune time for any major renovations to take place on our aging campus. We were in dire need of a new multipurpose room, so the construction for that had begun toward the end of the preceding school year. Our playground had been directly behind the old multipurpose room. When the old room was demolished, the playground was taken out, so there would be no playground until the completion of the new one.

Everything for the new playground had been completed except one minor detail. The construction company had not been back to inspect the new playground to be sure that no building materials, metal, or glass were left in the area, so the playground was not deemed safe. Someone was supposed to have come back to our school the preceding week, but no one had yet. There was still the blacktop area for basketball and tetherball, but that equipment was usually monopolized by the "big" kids, so my students and many other students had nothing to do after lunch. That thought sparked a question: "Do you all get bored at lunch recess?" They all responded with a resounding "Yes!" I went to the front board and wrote the word *playground*. I asked the students to let their minds wander and then say what they thought of when they heard that word and what it might have to do with all the problems that kept occurring during lunch.

Here are a few of the responses I was given: "Playgrounds are fun." "Kids need a playground." "We want swings." "We need to play." "We want the bridge back." "Please make it safe." "When we are bored, we get in trouble."

I never doubted them for a split second. It was myself that I doubted. Could I follow the process? Would I allow them to take control? Was I setting them up for failure? I had so many questions and misgivings. I decided to take a deep breath and trust the process. "So what are you all going to do to change this?" Despite my experience in asking this question about the library, I was not prepared for their response. They sat there and stared at me. Their faces displayed looks of confusion and fear. I think I also heard a few giggles in their midst. I asked them again what they could do to change the situation. Finally, Kimmi spoke up: "Us? What can we do? We are just kids." In agreement, James stated matter-of-factly, "Yeah, they won't listen to us. We can't tell adults what to do." I noticed the others nodding their heads in agreement with those two statements. At first, I felt saddened and scared. To think that at six and seven years of age, these students already believed they were powerless to make change.

I continued, "You know, I could talk to the principal and see what can be done, but guess what? This isn't affecting me like it is all of you. I think it would be best if the news came from the people who are being affected by the situation. You don't realize how much power you really have." Audible gasps could be heard. I went on: "Think about the authors we have studied and how they use words to change people's minds, to convince them of something. That is the kind of power I am talking about."

I reminded the students of all the persuasive books we had read and asked them to think of how the characters tried to get other people to change their mind in the stories. "Did they beg? Did they tell them they *had* to change their way of thinking? Did they disrespect the other people in the story? No! What did they do? They gave reasons to prove their point."

At this point in the conversation, the Social Action process wasn't in the forefront of my mind. We had covered the "what" and "why" parts of the process. Instead of thinking about the steps, I did what seemed like the next natural step, and it turned out that I was following the Social Action process. I was considering how to take action. We brainstormed about how we could change the situation. I recorded the students' ideas as they voiced them. No matter what the idea was, it was written on the white board. It was suggested that we talk to many people: our principal, the mayor, the janitor, the people who needed to inspect the playground, the construction men. After the suggestions, a discussion followed about who would be the logical choice. We voted on it, and the decision was reached to contact the construction men.

How were we going to do this? Again, we had a brainstorming session about our options. A few of the suggestions were call the company, tell the principal to talk to them, go to their office, or write them letters. Another conversation ensued. Sadie said that talking to the principal wasn't a good idea because we would be asking her to fix our problem for us. (Yay!) We voted in favor of writing letters to the construction men. Before writing the letters, we shared ideas about what we could write to the construction men to convince them that the playground was badly needed by the students at our school.

The letters were written, copied, and delivered to the construction company. Every day after that, my students came to school to see if their playground was ready. I reminded them that sometimes change takes a little bit of time and a lot of patience. They didn't have to wait for too long. Within that week, their playground was inspected, deemed safe, and reopened to the students.

I'll never forget picking up my students at the end of the after-lunch recess on the day after the playground reopened. They were beaming, so proud of what *they* had done. I looked at them and said, "See how much power you really do have." Emma said, "Yep, I guess you were right. They did listen to us."

I will always view the "playground day" as a major milestone in my teaching career. What is really encouraging to me is how my students are now so much more at ease with thinking of themselves as agents of change.

These experiences have been life-changing events for me. At the Social Action retreat in Santa Fe, New Mexico, my eyes were opened to a set of principles and a process for change that I had been thirsting for, without being aware of this need. I am not sure the library incident or the issue with the playground would have unfolded the way it did without me having knowledge of this process. When I returned from the retreat, I became more cognizant of opportunities for my students' voices rather than mine to be heard. I reflected on situations in which I should have stifled my voice. It's not as if my participation in this retreat made me suddenly able to see every opportunity to use the Social Action process or take every problem through that process. But I was definitely more deliberate about how I approached problematic situations. I was no longer *the* problem solver in the classroom; I was just one of twenty.

Lending Student Voice to Curriculum Planning

DIETTA POSTON HITCHCOCK

The previous year had been a doozy! No Child Left Behind initiatives reached the Roswell Independent School District in a big way. No classroom in our rural New Mexico town of fifty thousand had been left unscathed by sweeping changes, mandatory programs, and top-down philosophical shifts. In an effort to improve standardized test scores, computer testing became a weekly or even, at times, daily event, and mandatory significant blocks of core class time were spent on test subject matter. The curriculum of enrichment that I had taken for granted in my combined seventh- and eighth-grade gifted language arts class was no longer a given, and the natural rhythm of my teaching had been disrupted. Imposed programs and administrative constraints kept us in the classroom instead of pursuing our usual "let's go and find out" adventures in the community.

Even the group of students I was working with had changed dramatically. Though I was allowed to keep a class of only twelve students, the administration required full inclusion for the first time. We ended up with a combination class of three profoundly gifted students, three gifted students, and six regular education students. While I continued to teach an enriched curriculum, I had to reconcile my practice with the new "skill, drill, and test" mandates for each level of student, and I had had an internal battle all year, trying to fit everything in. By the spring,

I felt powerless and believed that I had failed my students. However, because I knew I would have these same students back the following year, I felt a reprieve.

In the fall, I decided to begin anew by including this new class in the process of planning their curriculum for the next year. Planning alongside my students would be a first step toward exercising more control over our educational environment. I knew that *I* had been affected by district changes, and there had been a great deal of grumbling from teachers and administrators throughout the previous year. I assumed that the students shared our concerns.

I had used parts of the Social Action process in another class to facilitate discussions, so I knew that the flexible activities would provide my new class with an opportunity to define and solve problems involving issues important to us. I had internalized the Social Action principle that "All people have skills, experience, and understanding that they can draw on to tackle the problems they face." I reminded myself that students know what they need, but are rarely asked.

The process begins with deciding *what* the issue is, and my class spent a lengthy amount of time—about a week—waxing the *what*. In their journals over the course of the year, the students responded to prompts that I posed, such as "Tell me about your year in this classroom" and "What do you think about the school district's changes this year, and how have they affected you and your learning?" By writing their answers, sharing in groups, and coming to consensus on answers with others, they slowly illuminated the issues that we would explore and address in our curriculum planning for the following year.

Throughout the year, students expressed their opinions on a zillion topics in comments ranging from "This has been the biggest learning year for me in this classroom" to "I hate reading out loud" to "I like this class because there's only one 'popular' kid in the room." Students were divided, but there were recurring themes. Our longest project, writing historical fiction short stories, was referred to with delight *and* hatred. Journal writing, it was noted, helped writing skills—and was torture.

Overwhelmed with so much information, I asked students to work in randomly assembled groups with chart paper and markers to categorize their own observations about the year in positive and negative lists. Working from these lists, I acted as a scribe at the board and wrote down items that the whole class could agree on as a positive or a negative. Was I in for an earful! I learned that day never to ask my students what they think unless I am prepared to hear the kinds of truths that are the most difficult to accept. I also learned that these difficult truths tend to be the most valuable.

One thing that I did *not* hear was an outpouring of dissatisfaction with the school district's new programs. Students commented on the frequent testing and daily skill reinforcement time, but they seemed to be equally divided between the opinion that "weekly testing stinks" and the opinion that "it has been helpful." The students did not vilify the school district. The notion of testing was not what upset them; it was the inappropriateness of content and the time taken away from their learning that bothered them.

At this point, I felt a little lost in my research. I realized that I had been counting on the students to share my strong negative feelings about the new classroom requirements. It struck me that my students were speaking the truth about themselves and that I hadn't been ready to listen. All year, I had been grumbling about our administration's use of data to say what the administration wanted the public to hear, regardless of the truth in the matter, and here I was trying to make my students' answers fit my neat and tidy premise! After the students left class, I collected their group notes so that I could look them over later. Then I went home and crawled into bed to sulk and chew on what had taken place.

I left the positive and negative items on the board for the next meeting while the students did the Movie Poster activity (see the activities in Part Three) in small groups. The poster that each group created was to be a metaphor for our class experience. I gave them the example of "The Attack of the Fifty-Foot Woman" to lend a sense of humor to the project.

The students worked on their posters for most of two class periods and finally presented them. A volunteer spokesperson from each group explained its choice of text and images to the class. One group parodied the World Wrestling Association with the title, "WLA: World Language Arts." Under the title, they drew an inset that said "Writing Gone Wrong!" next to an illustration of class mayhem. Under the drawing, a caption read: "During this year, we have gone through a lot of wrestling in language arts. We have had 'fish' fights, spit wad wars and the 'wrestling chair.' We have all been involved in this madness of a classroom, but have learned a lot, as well as in our stories."

Another group's poster was called "The Attack of the Short Stories" and subtitled "Evil Coffee Drinker trying to help or hurt?" A giant pencil was surrounded by tiny students screaming in pain while being whipped with a Cat o' Nine Tails by their teacher (me, I presume). The third poster spoofed *The Sound of Music* with "The Sound of Writing." A movie rating of "XXR" was drawn in the bottom right corner with a key that read "For violence, language, and disturbing images."

As I listened to each presentation, I could see for the first time since the beginning of the year that we had truly evolved into a unified group, with all of our differences and quirks intact. Still, I could not deny a disturbing common denominator in all three posters. Everyone recognized class behavior as a memorable issue.

Drawing on all of my students' responses, including those in their journals from these four days, I created a list of blanket statements, including "I learn more through activities that are hands-on," "Testing is helpful to my learning," "I love to write," "I hate to write," "Writing is a necessary evil," and "Mrs. H talks too much." We used them to do a modified version of the Four Faces activity (see Part Three) in which people showed their support for or disagreement with an idea by walking to a specific part of the room. Toward the end of this class period, one student piped up, "This is fun! We could use this to help us write persuasive essays!"

We had addressed the *why* stage naturally in our work on *what* and were ready to move to *how,* to address the question of what should be our main objective for the next year. I asked the students to brainstorm one goal that would encompass all that we had talked about in the last several class periods. After less than a minute, they decided: "Develop into better writers." I was thrilled to hear my students come up with and unanimously agree on this one statement.

To strategize about how we would do this, we used the Force Field Analysis activity (see Part Three). In the center of a large piece of chart paper, I wrote "Develop into Better Writers." As scribe, I wrote what students blurted out for positive actions, such as "solve behavior," "teach mechanics tailored to student needs," and "essays tied to projects of personal interest." They came up with only one phrase below the line to indicate what would not help them become better writers—"worksheets." Students shared their opinion that if we were working on something meaningful to them and "real," they would be less likely to have behavior problems. They wanted to go out into the community and do something that mattered—while improving their writing and learning new things. We agreed that we would not only develop research and writing skills by going on field trips linked to a large project in the community but also meet the New Mexico Standards and Benchmarks.

One of the concrete plans we made was to compact instruction on grammar and writing conventions at the beginning of the next year by making a class reference book. Another was a plan to do a long-term project with the local historical museum. As we brainstormed projects, I mentioned that the museum was looking for ways to bring the area's history into schools, and my students added it to our list of ideas.

I arranged to work with the museum in the next year. The director was ecstatic about our ideas and offered opportunities to explore the museum's collection, talk with their experts, and share artifacts. We talked about creating trunk shows to take around to elementary schools. The shows would be designed by my students and based on the interests they developed through their investigations at the museum. By the end of the school year, our planning work had prepared us to move to the *act* stage when the next school year started and, finally, to *reflect* on all that we had done and learned.

Fast-forward to winter of the next year.

As I conclude this piece, my students and I are finally poised to begin our project with the historical museum. All year, as we have tackled the ever-interrupting testing demons, the fine points of grammar, and persuasive writing, I have reminded my students that we are indeed headed for *our* project. In preparation, we have taken on some of the mini-projects we planned, such as expediting our nuts-and-bolts writing lessons by making our handbook: *Writing Bible—Everything You Need to Know to Write Well.*

The dynamics of our classroom have changed considerably. My students are aware of what they must learn as prescribed by the district, but in my class they have a say in *how* they learn. My students no longer perceive each assignment as arbitrary, but question me if they think it might be. Perhaps as a result, our discipline issues are better resolved and complaints about class work are at an all-time low. I am increasingly comfortable with giving students more freedom to work in groups and on their own.

Using Social Action with my students not only renewed my excitement as a teacher but also provided a learning experience suited to our classroom mandate. The Social Action process works comfortably with other educational methods, including the Autonomous Learner Model, the curricular model of my school's gifted department. Thus, our department strives to develop students who "solve problems or develop new ideas . . . with minimal external guidance in selected areas of endeavor" (Betts and Kercher, 1999, p. 12). In line with this, Social Action encourages students to take ownership of their own education and design their own Individualized Education Plans.

In writing their daily responses to our work, students also employ the six highest-order thinking skills of Bloom's Taxonomy: knowledge, comprehension, application, analysis, synthesis, and evaluation (Huitt, 2000). In these writings, the students analyze and synthesize our group process. During our discussions, the students express themselves, agree, disagree, and listen to others, forming a more purposeful and cohesive class community. We are now set to tackle academically focused language arts but also to delve into a literacy of place, a literacy of our own history, and a literacy of self—with a little help from Social Action.

The Story of the Youth Dreamers

In Their Own Words

**MILDRED HARRIS, CHANTEL MORANT, SHANTA CRIPPEN,
CHRIS LAWSON, CHEKANA REID, CIERRA CARY, TIFFANI YOUNG-SMITH**

WHO WE ARE (*WHAT* & *WHY*)

We are the Youth Dreamers, a group of young people between the ages of eleven and fifteen who share the same goals. We want to make our voices heard, help our community, and be a part of making a future for the youth of today. The Youth Dreamers are part of the Stadium School, a Baltimore City public school that serves about 140 students in grades four through eight from the communities surrounding Memorial Stadium. The Youth Dreamers originated in an elective course called Community Action in March 2001. Many of us are now in high school but continue to be involved.

---

*Never doubt that a small group of thoughtful,
committed citizens can change the world. Indeed,
it's the only thing that ever has.*
— Margaret Mead

When we started this project, we talked a lot about issues in the community. We decided that one of the issues that really bothered us was that too many young people get involved with negative activities after school. We also read that after school, many kids just hang out with nothing to do, and that this lack of structured activity can lead to bad grades, bad school attendance, drug abuse, and bad behavior.

25

Once we agreed that the lack of positive activities for kids was a community issue that we wanted to change, we did the But Why? activity (see Part Three) and brainstormed why kids getting involved in negative behavior was a problem for us and what the causes of the problem were. From our list, we decided that one thing we could change was the fact that young people don't have many safe, stimulating places to go after school. We would solve this smaller problem by creating a youth-run youth center. We hoped to keep kids off the street and maybe change their lives by removing drugs, violence, and other negative influences.

If you were to look us up in the dictionary, you might find this definition that we created together: "The Youth Dreamers: n. a group of young adults committed to decreasing negativity among their peers in the community by creating a safe, stimulating environment for personal and educational growth."

THE BEGINNING (*HOW* & *ACT*)

We decided that we wanted a youth center run by two adult directors, a board of directors that includes youth and adults, up to twenty-three teenagers in grades seven through twelve, at least eight adult volunteers from the community, Ameri-Corps volunteers, and a janitor. The teenagers would tutor members and teach a variety of classes along with adult volunteers. The center would include a variety of classes, such as sewing, pottery, mosaics, art, cooking, and typing.

Each teenager would commit to working at the center for a certain number of hours each week. They would be paid a small stipend for half of these hours and earn service learning hours for the other half. Adult volunteers would be paid a small stipend for their hours. The directors and janitor would be paid a set yearly salary. Finally, we were trying to set up a scholarship fund for Youth Dreamers who serve on the board of directors.

Not only would the center serve kids, it would also serve other community members. We would host block parties, open houses, neighborhood cleanups, and other activities that bring young people and adults together in positive ways.

The first thing we did to reach these goals was to write a pledge to show our commitment. "We pledge to persevere, knowing that this will take time; have patience as we believe in each other and support each other; face obstacles with courage; and take pride in our successes and learn from our failures." We decided that if someone decided to leave, they would be responsible for finding a replacement. Next, we wrote a business proposal that includes a one-year budget of operating costs. The budget took a long time to complete because we had to do a lot of research about how much monthly expenses cost, how much it would cost to buy and renovate a house, and so on.

Then we began a letter-writing campaign. We wrote lots of letters to our mayor and other government officials, the Department of Public Housing, the Orioles baseball team, the Ravens football team, and some reporters at our local paper. We wrote more than forty letters and received only three replies. We did not stop. We kept on writing, and though some did not hear us, we kept on fighting to be heard.

In the meantime, we had lots of bake sales at lunchtime. We raised about $200. We participated in an assembly at school to share what we were doing with all the other students. We wrote a rap for the assembly. We still sing the rap today. At the end of the year, we had a T-shirt fundraiser for the eighth-grade students who were leaving the school. On the T-shirts, we put iron-on pictures we had taken of their friends. Then we decorated the shirts with writing and rhinestones. The first roll of pictures that we took did not come out. This was two days before the last day of school! So we had to retake all the pictures, run to the drugstore to drop off the film, run back after school to pick up the pictures, and then iron and decorate until about 7:00 P.M., when we finally had all of our orders done! Whew! We worked hard!

Our first official funding was from Youth as Resources. We wrote a ten-page grant proposal requesting $3,000 for furniture for our center. We presented the grant over spring break to the Youth as Resources board of teens and adults. We were all nervous because we had never presented to a board. We were so proud when we got the money.

During the first summer of our project, our teacher called us to tell us that we were part of a federal bill by Senator Mikulski! She was the third person to respond to our letters! The bill set aside $70,000 for our youth center. We said things like "Wow!" "Oh my gosh! After all those letters!" "It's about time!" We finally had our dream come true, but we knew that this was only the beginning.

We organized a luncheon at which the senator would hand over the check. At the ceremony, she read aloud part of our letter and told us how impressed she was that we had been able to problem solve our T-shirt disaster. She partnered us with St. Ambrose Housing Aid Center to help us buy the house and with Habitat for Humanity to help us renovate the house. Since then, we have written many other grant proposals and now have over $180,000 toward our one-year operating budget of $276,000. Even though we were rejected by some foundations, we still kept writing and never gave up.

THROUGH THE YEARS (*HOW, ACT, REFLECT*)

During our years as Youth Dreamers, we have successfully completed many fundraisers in order to add to our budget. We have had benefit basketball games, bake sales, a penny drive, T-shirt sales, a talent show, a picture day, and a marathon fundraiser when our teacher ran the Boston Marathon. Each year that we have held the picture day fundraiser, we have gotten better at organizing, planning, and running it. All of these fundraisers have certain problems, but we wrote them down so that we will know how to do better the next time.

We have been involved in many presentations to spread the word. We have presented at Towson University and Villa Julie College. We have also presented for the Maryland Bankers Reinvestment Group, the University of Maryland's Law Clinic, Councilwoman Lisa Stancil, Youth as Resources, Youth Venture, and community groups. We have led workshops for middle school students in Baltimore City. We even organized a luncheon for potential funders so that they could see what we are trying to do. We presented our proposal at the Baltimore City Council meeting because we were invited to do so by Councilwoman Lisa Stancil. We have also gone on many site visits to other community groups to find out how they got started and how they do fundraising.

We have been on two different newscasts and on the radio. We were on stations all over the country when we won the Angel Soft Angels in the Classroom Award. At the ceremony, Jane Kaczmarek from *Malcolm in the Middle* donated an extra $10,000 from her family for our center. Last summer, Angel Soft came to film us for an educational documentary they are making to inspire students to do community work.

IN THE COMMUNITY

We have begun going to area elementary schools during the day to work with students who may be our future members. This is part of how we are going to recruit members for our center. We wrote letters to the principals to get permission and then planned activities and lessons to do with the younger children. Working with younger children is hard, but it pays off in the end.

Each year, we work with the Baltimore Community Foundation to review proposals for after-school programming in Baltimore. This is a long and hard process, but it gives us a chance to see how proposals are viewed from the "other side." One year, we also ran workshops for other middle school students in the city. We helped them identify problems in their community that they wanted to solve. We will continue to work with them, giving them advice and helping with their projects. Finally, we organized and planned an event called Interaction Festival for National Join Hands Day. Join Hands Day is an annual day of service that develops relationships between kids and adults through neighborhood volunteering.

NEXT STEPS

Toward the end of our second year, we did a lot of research on becoming a non-profit organization, and that June, we voted 16–1 to go ahead with it. By August, thanks to the University of Maryland's Free Law Clinic, we had become the Stadium School Youth Dreamers, Inc. We have a board of directors that has seven kids and seven adults. We spent that entire summer rewriting the bylaws and revising our mission statement. There are both youth and adult officers on our board, and we meet once a month.

Every new school year, Ms. Kristina gives seasoned Youth Dreamers the opportunity to teach the fresh Youth Dreamers what we have learned in past years. We have to do many different lessons on subjects like fundraising, talking on the telephone, working in elementary schools, budgeting and balancing a checkbook, and presentations. It takes us a lot of time to set it all up, especially since we try to make the lessons fun because kids can easily be distracted. Most of the fresh Youth Dreamers think this is a more effective way of teaching because they relate to their peers more than their teachers. Being a Youth Dreamer gives you opportunities to do things you would not usually do.

As far as getting our house, we have found the perfect one and are about to buy it. It is in horrible condition, but we have help from a Housing Aid Center to renovate and an architect who is working with us for free to sketch out the rooms. We have learned how to file a zoning appeal and are waiting for our hearing date. We have canvassed the neighborhood to get support for the change and to recruit members and volunteers. Plus, we have written to several TV shows that fix up homes and challenged them to take on our project. Finally, we wrote to lots of corporations like Home Depot to ask them to donate materials.

REFLECTIONS (OBVIOUS!)

We have learned a lot over the past three years. When we started, we didn't realize that this project would be so much work and take so much time. We have had to spend a lot of time—in school, after school, and on weekends—working. Some of our biggest challenges were not staying on task, getting responses, being comfortable presenting, and staying committed. But we have benefited because we have learned how to write grant proposals and letters and plan and run fundraisers, and we have learned from our mistakes. Most important, we have learned that if we stay committed, we can accomplish a lot by working together. When we thought we would have to give up on our dream home because it was in such bad shape and would cost so much, one of us said, "We didn't get this far by giving up." That inspired us to launch a campaign called "40 Days to $100,000," and even though we raised only $12,000, we got a lot of community support, and that is how we got our free architect. We have become good problem solvers, and we know how to reflect on our work to make it better.

The most exciting part of this whole experience has been seeing the things we want to happen actually happen, like getting our bill passed. We hope that other areas in our city will develop youth centers in their communities, which we hope will decrease crimes committed by teens. We hope that the newspapers and TV, which talk about bad stuff too much, will see the positive sides of Baltimore. We would like to see less young people on the corner and more going to college and becoming successful because of our project. Some people have become more positive about us, but we still have to deal with some adults' negative attitudes toward us. Sometimes they think that this is just a cute project and don't take us seriously, but we want our youth center to be known nationally for its outstanding achievements, accomplished totally by the young people in Youth Dreamers.

Reflections on the Youth Dreamers

KRISTINA BERDAN

When nine of my Baltimore City middle school students decided to create a freestanding youth-run youth center, I actually encouraged them to pick a smaller project. Although I had done
successful community projects with other students and had attended
several training sessions with the Centre for Social Action, I did not
see how students were going to be able to mobilize to raise the money
and garner the support to do what no other youth group had done
on their own. Having taught many of these students and having seen
how easily frustrated they were at having to revise a paper, I doubted
that they had the staying power to stick it out for the years that it
would take to accomplish this task. It took little time for me to realize that they were going to do exactly that. Through their own efforts,
the Youth Dreamers are on the road to seeing their dream become a
reality.

In the beginning, I could never have predicted how enormous this project
would become or how much I would struggle with my role as teacher-facilitator.
When I announced Community Action as my elective course, I noted a low collective groan among the students. Only nine courageous souls signed up for the
course, choosing to give up the chance to play basketball, football, or African
drums. We began by really talking about the issues in their community that bothered them. The students clearly enjoyed being given the opportunity not only to

talk in class but also to talk about their interests, not the interests of the curriculum writers in their district. When asked to focus on one issue, the students unanimously agreed on the issue of teenagers being on the streets and involved in violent activities after school hours. From that point, I guided the students into thinking about why this problem exists. Using the But Why? activity (see Part Three) and additional discussion, the students decided to tackle "teenagers on the street after school is a problem because they have nowhere safe to go and they are bored." The idea of a youth-run youth center was born, and although I did my best to encourage them to take on a smaller project, they were now united and determined. We signed a pledge to commit to the project, and I felt like I had signed my life away.

If you have an idea, even if you think it's stupid,
voice your opinion! Be bold! That's what
Youth Dreamers is all about!
— Astarte

During my elective course, I created instant mini-lessons based on needs that arose during class. As time progressed, I couldn't help but notice the tremendous number of skills the students were learning and applying. Students were enthusiastically writing business proposals, grants, budgets, and letters of inquiry to foundations. They were planning and executing presentations, making site visits to interview directors of other youth centers, and organizing meetings of adults and youths. They were planning fundraisers, evaluating them, and calculating their profit. It was a thrill to see the real-world connections and application of skills from other classes that these students were demonstrating every day. But there was never enough time at the end of the day, and I was tired of always meeting after school. This was real learning that should be given more of a place in the daily schedule. I had to speak to the staff. This had to be more than an elective class. But would they agree? And how would we do it?

Fortunately, I work in a New School Initiative school, a Baltimore City public school run by teachers, parents, community members, and students. While we are constrained by the city budget and city and state testing mandates, we are able to write our own curriculum, create our own schedules, determine our own class sizes, and so on. Because of my participation in numerous Social Action training sessions through the collaboration of the National Writing Project and the Centre for Social Action, I felt qualified to continue with Social Action in my classroom on a much larger scale. I decided to approach the staff in order to share my knowledge of Social Action and my experiences with it in the classroom. When I spoke to them about what I had observed in my Community Action elective course, they were enthusiastic about taking that class to a different level and taking other projects in the school to that level, too. Together we decided to create more class time by devoting a full day each week to "Project Day." In addition, each teacher created a "project class" with activities linked directly to the community, such as organizing events, creating a community gardening project, or bringing in community artists to work with students. Once we'd made these decisions, we set to work writing curricula for the classes.

This class is different because in Youth Dreamers,
we are making change in the community.
— Chekana

I noticed a phenomenal transformation in my project class in comparison with my seventh-grade English class. In my English class, students refused to write a short story, but the Youth Dreamers would write ten-page grants. In my English class, I would come up with creative, interactive ways to teach students how to address an envelope and notice that whenever they needed to do so, they were unable to do it correctly. Switch to the Youth Dreamers class, in which a student pulled me aside to ask how to address an envelope. I showed her once; she filled out the envelope that held the grant that went to the foundation, and I never had to show her again. In my English class, asking a student to revise a paper became an emotional disaster. In Youth Dreamers, students would come to me to ask if they had left out any important information in their letter of inquiry to a foundation. When rejection letters rolled in, I would prepare myself with Winston Churchill quotes ("Success is nothing but failure after failure with undiminished enthusiasm"), but the students would look at me and then ask, "So who should we write to next?" This was an aberration from the English classroom, where the students would fall apart if they did not receive the grade they expected on a paper.

In my English class, students constantly bickered over trivial matters, fought for attention, and rarely respected the contributions of others. In the Youth Dreamers class, students would democratically decide who would get to be the one student who was interviewed on the morning news. On one occasion, I had stayed up the previous night, desperately trying to think of a democratic way to choose the representative. The students responded to the situation with comments such as "I'm not really comfortable being on the news; I am way too nervous"; "I don't think I am the best representative because I have only been with the Youth Dreamers a few months"; "I'm not sure I would be able to answer all the questions confidently"; and "Well, I really think that since Chantel has been involved since the beginning and is really good at public speaking, she should do it." As a class, they decided to each write down their top three choices for a representative, and they tallied the votes to come up with one representative and a runner-up. These two students worked together to prepare for questions that might come their way. In addition, the students would recognize the strengths and contributions of others when deciding on mini-project groups.

At one point, I had students begging to be part of the Youth Dreamers, particularly students who did not typically work very hard in regular classes. One of my English/language arts students who did very little work in class asked whether he could join. I responded with, "It's a lot of hard work, and you don't do very much work in class." He surprised me when he said, "But Youth Dreamers is important. They're really doing something." I didn't know whether to be upset at the notion that he thought we weren't really doing "something" in English class or thrilled at the realization that he saw the Youth Dreamers as a group of students taking responsibility for making positive change in their world.

Individual students in the Youth Dreamers were baffling me. LaTanya was failing all of her other classes but was the leader in the Youth Dreamers, organizing and running fundraisers, starting a group to plan and run the talent show, and writing a five-page grant to have a block party in the community. Students were choosing to stay after school in order to plan a presentation. Instead of bemoaning the schoolwide Halloween party that only raised $5 for the Youth Dreamers, we decided during our reflections that it showed what good planners we were and that we could organize and control a whole student body on a holiday. We moved it from the fundraising part of our budget and included it in reports for funders to show these strengths. Again, negative attitudes seemed to evaporate, and enthusiasm took their place. I stayed up nights, wondering, What is happening here? Why is it happening here? Why isn't it happening in my English/language arts class? Is it going to go away? Should I not talk about it for fear of it going away? Should I ask them about it? Is it just a case of luck or magic? I was constantly pondering these questions, to help me better understand both the effects of Social Action and what I was doing wrong in my regular classroom.

What I came to realize was that students come to my Community Action elective course by choice, which is very different from how students come to my English class. Students are in my English class because they are forced to be there. They are learning what is prescribed by the city, not necessarily what they want to learn. For the most part, I am teaching what I am told to teach, not what I can see they need to learn.

With the Youth Dreamers, I am a Social Action worker using the skills I have as a teacher to help facilitate a student-chosen goal. The students have identified the issues, brainstormed why the problems exist, decided how they are going to address them, taken action, and reflected on almost every step along the way. Unlike my traditional classroom, in which students have little control of their own learning, the Youth Dreamers have total ownership of what they are doing and why they are doing it. Every Wednesday, *they* decide what needs to be done and they do it. I provide the structure, but they are given the choice and most of the control.

I believe that I am no longer seen as their teacher, but more as a resource. This can be an uncomfortable role for me as a teacher to be in because I never know what will happen next, which direction the students will choose to go, or how they will handle the next challenge. Although I have given up the element of control that a traditional teacher holds, the structure of our days, the goals we have in common, and the desire to see a dream become a reality bring self-control to the classroom.

On Wednesdays, I am a Social Action worker working in the confines of the classroom. I use my skills as a teacher to provide mini-lessons and guidance, and grading is included. I am working with a group of students with a shared goal. The rest of the week, I am an English/language arts teacher, guided by the principles of Social Action and good teaching, incorporating these theories into my practice. I am working with a group of students with very different needs, no common goal, and a required curriculum.

> *If we can't go through trials, we can't*
> *move forward and be strong.*
> — Astarte

Working with Social Action in the classroom has provided me with a new set of challenges. Often, I lack credibility among my colleagues because of my role as facilitator and guide rather than traditional teacher. I also face adults who refuse to believe that this is a youth-led project; thus, they expect me to provide information or to do work that the youths typically do. The teacher in me often wants to jump in and fix things, even though I know full well that the most valuable lessons come from the youths doing the fixing, not to mention that they are the experts and the ones running the project. Finally, this project has taken on a life of its own and has taken over my life as I knew it. I was unprepared for any of these challenges, but trusting the process, the youths, what I know as a teacher, and what other Social Action colleagues can share has made it easier to deal with them.

> *We want our voice to be heard and to make change*
> *in the community. Sometimes adults underestimate us.*
> *But once they find out, they change their minds.*
> — Tiffani

The students face their own set of challenges and struggles. They have been discouraged by the attitude of adults who don't take them seriously because they are youths. They are frustrated by the media's portrayal of youths: "The newspapers and TV . . . talk about bad stuff too much. [The public needs to] see the positive sides of Baltimore." The students often have trouble staying on task, and they get irritated when students don't do their part: "The most frustrating thing is people not doing their job as a Youth Dreamer." Although they respond by writing more letters, students are frustrated "when we write letters to people and they don't write back." They, too, feel the effects of how much time this project has taken: "The thing that frustrated me was that things didn't happen right away. It took some time in school and after school. It seemed like we were going nowhere." Many have had trouble staying committed to the goal, while others have never strayed: "I have learned the importance of commitment and that all of us working together is better than doing it yourself." The lessons learned seem to overpower the frustrations. Seasoned Youth Dreamer Chekana says, "If you really want to do it, then do it. Don't give up. You may come across rejections, but keep going, never stop." And Fresh Youth Dreamer Zakiyah says, "We have to work hard for what we want. Everything is not easy. Things are not gonna land in our lap."

It is a privilege and an honor to be a member of the Youth Dreamers, Inc. Being a Youth Dreamer takes a lot of dedication, concentration, commitment, open-mindedness, and consideration.
— Zakiyah

Being so immersed in this project has made it difficult for me to step back and view what is happening in an objective way. Although I am overwhelmed by my own questions about this work and the struggles I see the students grappling with, what I do see is very clear.

I see the smile on Cierra's face when she finds out that she secured $20,240 worth of funding from a grant she wrote. I also see her mother bragging to a community member at our festival about how hard her daughter is working toward this dream. I see LaTanya walking around the classroom, wearing a huge grin after faxing her four-page grant, taunting, "What did you do today? Anything? I wrote an entire grant." I see Astarte running into the room, breathless after a call to the senator, exclaiming, "The bill is on the president's desk. He is going to sign it!" I see Shani sitting on a different board of adults and youths, helping to decide which after-school programs should get funding in the city.

I see adults and youths sitting around a table, adjusting bylaws so that they read not "President" and "Chairperson" but "President" and "Youth President" instead.

I see the amazement on Nathan's face when we get to Wal-Mart and are presented with an overflowing shopping cart of toys and craft supplies because of a letter he wrote to five corporate officials. I see Chris, Mildred, Chantel, and me on the other side of the table, now serving as Youth as Resources board members, not youth coming to ask for money. I see Jade smiling and sighing with relief after presenting her first workshop to middle school students in the Turn the Corner Achievement Program. I see the look of shock on Chekana's face when the Youth Dreamers are presented with a resolution from the Baltimore City Council after their presentation. I see sixteen students showing up for a meeting in the middle of the summer, enthusiastic about setting goals for the new year.

I see Chris, now two years into high school, at our monthly board meeting, responding to "Well, maybe some of the old board members will step down to make room for new ones" with "What? We started this, and we want to finish it!" I see Chantel presenting an amazing speech to the board in her bid to become their youth president, and I see Astarte following with an equally impressive speech and a copy of her résumé for all. I see e-mails like this one from Zakiyah: "This is soooooooooooooooo great that we are now officially called the Stadium School Youth Dreamers, Inc. I couldn't be more proud to say that I am a part of this outstanding, goal setting, accomplishment making group, the Youth Dreamers." That e-mail was followed by one from Tiffani after being elected to the board: "THANK YOU SO MUCH EVERYONE FOR LETTING ME HAVE A CHANCE TO BE ON THE BOARD. THANK YOU."

I see youths who have accomplished more at age thirteen than many people will accomplish in a lifetime. I see youths who, having written letters and grants, have written their ticket to college; youths who have been interviewed on television and on the radio; youths who have given presentations at major universities and in front of numerous groups of adults; youths who have researched and started their own nonprofit organization; and youths who have planned and run their own community block party. I see youths who are stakeholders in their community and who, I hope, will come back to serve their community in the future. I see youths who believe in their project and its lasting effects: "We would like to see less young people on the corner and more going to college and being successful because of our project." I see youths who truly believe that hard work and dedication make a difference: "We didn't get this far by giving up."

Ultimately, I see a group of students who embody the principles of Social Action, because they believe that they

- Have the skills, experience, and understanding to draw on to tackle problems they face
- Have the right to be heard, to define the issues facing them, and to take action on their own behalf
- Can work collectively and have power
- Can make decisions for themselves and take ownership of whatever outcome ensues

---

Before I joined the Youth Dreamers, I didn't think kids could do this stuff. But now I know that we can.
— Domonique

How does this fit into the curriculum? Following is a list of skills and knowledge that my classes have developed through the use of Social Action.

English and Language Arts
- Writing business letters
- Creating and filling out order forms
- Grant writing
- Writing proposals
- Writing thank-you notes
- Creating invitations
- Addressing envelopes
- Writing articles
- Writing press releases
- Keeping logs and journals
- Note taking
- Reading grant guidelines
- Reading newspapers

- Using the phone book
- Reading and comparing real estate listings
- Conducting research
- Writing reports for funders

Math

- Fundraising (tracking costs, calculating profit)
- Selling items (making change)
- Calculating yearly bills
- Creating a budget
- Calculating square footage of properties
- Calculating stipends and salaries for one year
- Estimating event costs
- Balancing a checkbook

Social Studies

- Government
  - Identifying representatives at the local, state, and federal levels
  - Studying how a bill becomes a law
  - Determining how to file a zoning appeal and proceed through the process of obtaining a zoning appeal
  - Obtaining permits for neighborhood events
- Studying historical examples of Social Action

Technology

- Searching for foundations and grants on the Web
- Researching housing listings online
- Creating mailing labels
- Creating business cards
- WordPerfect word processing
- Using Excel spreadsheets

- Designing and updating websites
- Working alongside an architect to design a house by revising electronic blue-prints

Real-World Skills
- Conducting site visits and interviews
- Conducting telephone research
- Becoming a nonprofit organization
- Making presentations and speaking in public
- Making TV and radio appearances
- Working with community groups
- Networking at community events
- Soliciting donations for annual silent auction
- Interviewing and hiring staff for after-school programs
- Training employees for after-school programs
- Planning, running, and evaluating after-school programs

Character
- Persistence
- Patience
- Positive attitudes in the face of obstacles
- Communication skills

Community Action in a Summer Writing Institute

CHINWE "LA TANYA" OBIJIOFOR

I refuse to be labeled as powerless, and I do not want my students to view themselves in that manner, either. Perhaps that is why I was so intrigued when the director of the Peachtree Urban Writing Project in Atlanta encouraged me to apply for the Social Action Summer Institute. My curiosity about Social Action led me to the Centre for Social Action's website to check out what they were about. As I skimmed the principles, phrases such as "challenge injustice and oppression" and "people also have the right to define themselves" resonated with me. At the Social Action Summer Institute, I learned about the complexities of the Social Action process and gained insight into how it might be used in real situations. That is why, after attending the Social Action institute, I decided to try to use the process in our Summer Writing Institute for Students (SWIS) the next summer.

Since its creation in 1999, the focus of SWIS has been on honing students' writing skills, examining African and African American heritage, promoting a positive self-image, and fostering peer cooperation. SWIS is a three-week institute that meets weekdays from 9:00 A.M. until 3:00 P.M. There are three or four teachers and a few teenage assistants working with fifteen to twenty students from grades three through five. SWIS is designed to promote a safe atmosphere that motivates and encourages students to write and express themselves through media such as journals, art, music, stories, and poetry. An important activity for team building is a daily Umoja (Unity) Circle, which is an opportunity for the students to make positive comments about themselves and others, critique the previous day, and resolve conflicts. We also engage in writers workshops, peer response groups, African dance, music classes, and field trips. The culminating activities are the publication of a student anthology and a closing program. Parents and community members are invited to this program, in which students read the writing pieces they have selected and perform an African dance. At the end of the program, each student is awarded a certificate.

That summer, our participants were an economically diverse group of twelve African American students aged eight through twelve. Some lived in subsidized housing in low-income neighborhoods; others lived in single-family homes in middle-class neighborhoods; and some resided in apartments. All of the young people lived in African American communities, except for one male who lived in an area that was predominantly white.

The students explored what *their issues, problems, and concerns were.* During the preliminary sessions before the official start of the program, the students brainstormed about issues that concerned them. One issue they mentioned was the prevalence of landfills in South DeKalb County, a predominantly black community. This may not seem like a concern that many elementary students would want to address. However, during the drive to the preliminary session, two of the participants had heard a radio program about the landfills in South DeKalb County, and they began to discuss it as a concern.

On the first day of the summer institute, students discussed the issues with each other and voted for the one that they would address. The students named a range of issues that were on their minds. For example, Trina and James had the following exchange:

TRINA: My issue is landfills because they are all in the black community and that's not right. . . .

JAMES: My issue is not enough recess. Kids work hard all day, thinking they're gonna get recess. And all they get is more work. That makes me feel sad. . . .

After the students met in small groups and presented concerns that were important to them, it was time to vote. The facilitators decided that we would conduct a secret ballot so that students would feel comfortable voting for what they really wanted. When the votes were tallied, we discovered there was a tie between landfills and not having recess at school. As Social Action facilitators, we had to decide what to do about the tie.

In making this decision, we took several factors into consideration. First, the daily meetings of SWIS were within two miles of the largest landfill in the state, which was under close government scrutiny for not following clean air regulations. We had all breathed the foul odors emanating from the landfill. Second, our proximity would enable us to visit the facility, interview the operators, and make firsthand observations. Finally, the location of the landfills was a major issue in the participants' communities, and if they wanted to, they could become part of a grassroots movement and gain experience in community organizing. I should also note that one of our biases was that we, the facilitators, all live near landfills, and some of us are activists and wanted to be involved in this issue ourselves. At this moment, the line between facilitator and participant was blurred.

Students examined why *the problem of landfills existed.* After we decided to address the concentration of landfills in the black community—specifically, in South DeKalb County—we explored possible causes. I began by placing the words "landfills in the black community" in a circle in the middle of a piece of chart paper. Then I asked the students why they thought the landfills were clustered in the black community. I took the first response, "Black neighborhoods are dirty," and placed it on a line that I had drawn coming from the circle. Then I asked them why they thought black communities were dirty, and someone said it was because during slavery, black people were not allowed to live in nice neighborhoods. I wrote that on a line that was attached to the first line. When a student said, "Black people are lazy," I began a new line because it represented a new idea. We continued in this manner until the students finished responding.

I was appalled at some of these responses and literally felt an ache in my heart, but I was not surprised. It was apparent that some of our children had internalized negative stereotypes about black people. However, some of the older students had profound insight. James and Aaliyah suggested that landfills are located in black communities because landfill owners think that black people are powerless to stop them, and that these owners respect white neighborhoods more. When I asked them why they felt that way, they said it was because the landfill owners were white and because of negative media images of black people. Trina made it perfectly clear that black people are *not* inferior to whites, but equal. After we did this activity, we engaged in a discussion about how people come to have negative attitudes about themselves and how these attitudes might be counteracted.

This experience made me think hard about a question that had been debated at the Social Action Summer Institute: Is it important or necessary for Social Action facilitators to come from the same community as the people that they are working with as participants? At SWIS that year, there were three African American teachers, as well as two African American assistants—a high school student and a college student. I wondered whether the participants would have aired their views so honestly about black neighborhoods being dirty or black people being lazy if the facilitators had been outsiders. I also wondered whether an outside facilitator would have felt comfortable addressing the issue of internalized self-hate or would have known which resources to use in this discussion. I believe that community members themselves have to be involved in facilitating Social Action projects. It cannot always be outsiders.

Now that the students understood why the problem existed, they were ready to decide how *they might be able to change things in a meaningful way.* After the But Why? activity (see Part Three) we watched *One Million Postcards,* a video about two eleven-year-old girls who worked together to end the United States' embargo against Iraq. This gave the children ideas about different types of activities they could develop. Then the students brainstormed and discussed suggestions for an action plan. After voting, they chose to make an informational brochure to pass out in the communities surrounding the landfills and to solicit a radio station to publicize their concerns. At the end of our first day, we visited Live Oak, the largest landfill in Georgia, which is partially in South DeKalb County and is one of eight in the area. Then we reflected on our activities in our journals.

Kiara wrote, "Today we worked on issues and voted on a topic. The topic we picked was landfills. We also went to a landfill nearby called Live Oak, it was our first field trip. The smell of the landfill wasn't so nice, I would put it in a way that it just stank. The sounds were screeching, just noises and it was full of dust. It was shocking to me that it looked very "pleasant" and "neat". Also let me add one more thing for the smell it was head aching and gross. Anyway it was a pretty nice field trip and pretty short."

We talked about propaganda, including different techniques. During the lesson, students selected a particular technique and dramatized it. The students predicted that when we returned to Live Oak for our guided tour, representatives would stack the cards by only pointing out positive aspects of the landfill, as a way of convincing us that Live Oak was a good corporate neighbor. And that is exactly what they did.

Tenaya wrote, "When we went to Live Oak Landfill, I think that they were going to bribe and card stack us. The reason why I think they were trying to bribe us is by giving us a cookie, a soda, and some other tokens. They were card stacking by telling us all the good things about the landfills and not the bad things about it. To me all the bad things were the smell and the way that they put dirt on the trash. And they tried to put trees like between the houses and the landfill so that people wouldn't see what was going on. It's bad things and good things about Live Oak Landfill."

Aaliyah wrote, "Today we took a tour of Live Oak Landfill. When we first got there they used two kinds of propaganda. First they buttered us up by giving us soda and cookies. Then they started stacking cards. I didn't hear them say one bad thing about their company. Then again the tour spoke for itself it was disgusting. Everywhere you looked there was trash. It may not look as if it were trash but it was tons and tons of trash."

The students spent the rest of the first week on researching landfills by using the Internet, reading newspaper articles, and interviewing knowledgeable people. They also went on field trips and wrote reflections. The students also worked on making individual story quilts, using any issue they chose.

In the second week, we returned to persuasive writing. I felt that we had left it hanging after the initial lesson, and I wanted the students to use it for an authentic purpose. I talked to them about our county commissioner, Lou Walker, and his decision not to support curbside recycling because of the additional cost to taxpayers. In DeKalb County, the sanitation department only picks up lawn clippings. Any other recycling requires a trip to the recycling center. Needless to say, that has not been successful, and DeKalb County has yet to reach the state mandated goal of a 25-percent reduction in garbage. They decided to write persuasive letters to Commissioner Walker, urging him to support curbside recycling. I think that one of the reasons they were eager to contact Walker was their discovery that 60 to 70 percent of the waste in landfills is recyclable. Their research led them to conclude that reducing and reusing our garbage would slow the need for landfill expansion. The students could not understand how money was more important than the community's health. Aaliyah's letter asked, "I know this would be a big dip in the citizens' financial budget, but is money more important than peoples' lives?"

Commissioner Walker responded to our letter. He applauded the children's initiative and interest in such an important public health matter but denied not supporting curbside recycling and suggested that we conduct more thorough research in the future.

The students took action. We began working with students in small groups. As we facilitated, the students alternated between developing their informational brochure, writing, and working on their story quilts. They also reviewed their research in preparation for a visit from Karim Shahid, a member of the South DeKalb Neighborhoods Coalition, the leading organization fighting local landfill expansion. He conducted a roundtable discussion with the students and was amazed at their knowledge. They were able to discuss the necessity of capturing and reusing methane gas and the danger of leachate seeping into the water supply. Because Shahid is developing an environmental education program, he asked for the students' input about what types of activities and content they felt would be important. He also invited them to enter a writing contest about landfills.

"Overwhelming" is the only way to describe the final week of the institute. We had to disseminate the brochures; we were making a video; and we had planned two major field trips—one to Birmingham and the other to an amusement park. Finally, the SWIS anthology had to be completed for the closing read-around. Although the video still needed final editing, we felt good about all that we had done to accomplish our goals. As I mentioned earlier, the school where we met for SWIS was less than two miles from the largest landfill in the state; so the students passed out their brochures in the community and talked to people about the issues. They also left a stack of brochures at the local library and the recreation center. The students were proud of being able to share their knowledge with people in the neighborhood!

At our read-around, parents and visitors were impressed with the students' knowledge of the issues surrounding landfills in South DeKalb County. Many of the parents commented on how much they had learned because of their children's involvement in SWIS. However, questions still remain as to whether the children will continue their involvement with the issue of landfills in the black community. Will this experience translate into proactive behavior in other aspects of their lives?

Experimenting with Social Action with the students in our summer institute taught us valuable lessons. Most important is that we must have faith in our children. However, we must also give them guidance and resources when they need them. The biggest tension between our traditional way of working and Social Action was figuring out when to step in and when to pull back. For example, we could allow the students to go around in circles about what to put in the brochure for only so long. We eventually used guiding questions to help the students articulate their purpose and decide what type of information they wanted to include. We also learned to make sure our schedule was doable. Because our preliminary session was squeezed into our summer session, we lost time for a very crucial component—the ending reflections. Unfortunately, we did not have enough time to allow the students to voice their opinions about the strengths and weaknesses of the program or to suggest next steps.

Social Action turned out to be a great fit with the Summer Writing Institute for Students. One of the teachers who had initially been skeptical about infusing SWIS with Social Action expanded the number of art pieces she uses to include art assignments that lend themselves to Social Action activities. She wrote, "I was so amazed at how the children took to this project. They absorbed so much information in such a short time. It's going to impact them for a long time."

Changing Our World

LORI FARIAS, CRITICS OF SOCIETY CLASS

Sparks High School is located in downtown Sparks, Nevada, the sister city of Reno. Minority students constitute over half of the school's student body, and the school has one of the district's highest percentages of students living in poverty. Critics of Society is a one-semester, untracked English class consisting of juniors and seniors. Before attending the Social Action Institute, I had developed the class into one that required students to "change the world." I came up with a syllabus that requires students to choose their own cause, research it, create a plan of action to positively affect the cause, act on it, reflect on their progress, and present their entire project to the class. This project is worth 50 percent of their semester grade. The rest of their grade comes from in-class readings and assignments.

I felt like I was onto something, but I just wasn't sure how to realize the idea's full potential. Then I was invited to a Social Action retreat. I hoped that Social Action would help me refine the class, and it did.

The "what" stage of the Social Action process gave me ideas on how to help students think about their world, to identify things they wanted to change. Before the institute, I just assumed that students would have issues in the forefront of their minds. Social Action helped me recognize that students, like me, need to have time to discover and define their concerns. Social Action also reemphasized for me the need to let students decide for themselves what they want to work on; I cannot censor or lead them to an issue. Because I am opinionated and because students sometimes choose to work on causes I don't believe in, this has not always been easy. Guided by the Social Action principles, which affirm the importance of student authority, I ask students to show that their cause is not hurting anyone else or infringing on others' rights, then I let them go.

The "why" stage fits beautifully with the research component of the project. I ask the students to become "experts" on their causes before deciding what to do about them. Often, students start with an idea of what they want to do, but in the research stage, which often involves interviews and community contacts, they discover other methods. Because of classroom time constraints, I have strayed a bit from the Social Action principle that "it is important to identify the reasons why [the issues] exist so that any solutions devised will attack root causes and not just symptoms." I do want my students to understand root causes, but if they choose to work to improve the lives of those suffering the symptoms, I do not mind. Within one semester, they often don't have the time to work on the root causes. We discuss this difference in class, and I hope that they will leave with the knowledge that with more time they could initiate greater change.

After research, the students write a declaration that defines their cause and states specifically what they intend to do about it: the "how" stage. I read these, and we discuss them as a group in an effort to determine possible roadblocks and dead ends. Sometimes students decide to continue with their plans even after we've discussed substantial roadblocks. For example, I had a student who was concerned about teen pregnancy. This student wanted to make other teens more aware of the dangers of unsafe sex. I explained to her that doing presentations in middle schools or even the high school was probably not going to happen, but she insisted on trying. In the end, she settled for making posters with statistics and quotes from teen parents. She was pleased that these were hung in every classroom on our campus, but she went through a lot of frustration and anger to arrive at her final success. I felt that I had to allow her to try, and Social Action gave me the philosophical foundation to do this.

Throughout the semester, I ask students to do weekly reflections on their projects, to consider what they've done, to review contacts they've made, and to explore their feelings as they run into problems or as they experience successes. I also require students to write a formal reflective essay that encapsulates the whole experience and explores what they've learned about each other, their cause, the world, and themselves in the world. Obviously, this phase of my project ties in nicely with the reflection stage of Social Action.

In the two years after the Social Action retreat, several students have received public acclaim for their projects, and we have earned a positive reputation in the school. Most important, I believe that the class has helped students learn about self-reliance.

The following collaborative article, written by the students, was published in *InLand: A Journal for Teachers of English Language Arts*. In the article, the Critics of Society, as my students named themselves, tell their story of the class and the change they perceive that they created and experienced. It is loosely modeled on an excerpt from Tim O'Brien's *The Things They Carried* (O'Brien, 1998), a book we read and used for an in-class assignment. The students chose this format for the piece and worked together to write, revise, and edit it.

—Lori Farias

CHANGING OUR WORLD

The changes we hoped to create were largely determined by our consciences, the paths we have taken, and the impact society has had on us. We were also driven to change the way adults perceive us, a diverse group of juniors and seniors from Sparks High. Perhaps because we are all aware of the realities and struggles of poverty, many of us wanted to help the poor around us. Jamie, Lily, and Jessica wanted to help a struggling single mother. James and Kaleb wanted to provide Christmas to one of the many homeless Sparks High families. Michael and Luke, basketball players who recognized that most of our students can't afford expensive camps and lessons, wanted to help incoming students improve their game in an affordable way. Katie has watched her aunt struggle with the expenses of having a child with cancer, so she teamed up with Gina and Liz to aid a similar family.

We all read pieces that made us think, made us cheer, made us mad. Among others, we have read Henry David Thoreau's "On Civil Disobedience," Jonathan Swift's "A Modest Proposal," Martin Luther King Junior's "Letter from the Birmingham Jail," and Hermann Hesse's *Siddhartha* (Hesse, 1982). We also listened to each other's writings. Ana shared a view of reality not often discussed, a view of a little girl horribly abused, a view that brought stunned silence and tears. Theresa then united with Anika, Dana, Jennifer, Trudy, and Denise, who, driven by their own experiences, wanted to change the lives of those living in violent situations. Melissa shared a memory of her Native American grandmother that helped the rest of us understand her culture, and then she decided to do the same in the wider community.

We debated many topics—topics that are often taboo in school, topics that directly impact our lives: same-sex marriage, government and institutional corruption, gender roles, abortion, racism, sexuality. Michelle wanted to do something to help prevent teen pregnancy and STDs. Peter and David, who constantly stand up for our government, wanted to let veterans know that teenagers respect their sacrifices. Lupe told us about her experience as a Latina and chose to change the experiences of other Latino students.

In the process of trying to change our world, we all ran into obstacles that slowed our projects and, periodically, brought them to a standstill. Every group had to deal with unfamiliar procedures—the school's typical red tape, local stores' and corporations' requirements, confidentiality laws. All of us became very familiar with gatekeepers and learned the importance of persistence. While Michael and Luke were attempting to contact middle schools to find a location for their basketball camp, the schools' office staffs often discarded them as undedicated teenagers. We decided early on that, no matter how difficult, we were going to stick to our hopes of changing the world.

We worked for hours outside of class, arranging meetings with our groups, waiting for unreturned phone calls, writing letters requesting donations and then delivering the letters to unresponsive store clerks and managers, creating posters and flyers, and buying supplies. Liz, Gina, and Katie baked dozens of cookies to sell each day at nutrition break; they also made birdhouses to sell. After all this, the girls met weekly with Jake, who is three years old and suffering with brain cancer, to play with him, to read to him, to give his mom a break.

Although some of us didn't reach our original goals, we all believe we have changed the world. We've raised over seven hundred and fifty dollars to donate to families in need. We not only directly changed three families' Christmas celebrations, we also showed the families that others care and there is hope. Jessica, Jamie, and Lily met with a single mother, Ms. Smith, who is battling cancer. She has four children (including twins who are eight years old) and her house recently burned down. The girls met with Ms. Smith and she said that above everything she was worried about her children at Christmas. Through a raffle, the girls raised money to help her buy gifts for her children. Ms. Smith couldn't believe that three seventeen-year-old girls would go out of their way to help a stranger. They did; now she believes.

In our quest to change the world, some of us spent time with young people. Melissa spent thirty hours working with a Brownie troop—fifteen eight-year-olds and one five-year-old; she plans on continuing through the school year. Melissa taught the troop the importance of heritage while providing a positive teen role model. She changed their lives two hours at a time. Michael and Luke worked with eighth graders, showing them techniques on the basketball court while also showing them that "high schoolers" are concerned, dedicated students. Sarah volunteered at a family education center. She spent over forty hours cleaning toys, working in the office, playing with children, doing whatever she could to help.

We believed in ourselves. We believed that we all had the power to change the world. We knew there needed to be a change, but we didn't know that one of the biggest changes would occur within us. Some of us changed our own minds during the process of changing others. James, who ended up raising money for a homeless family, originally thought all homeless people were lazy and undeserving of help. He now worries about the many homeless children who are unable to change their situations. Those of us who teamed up against domestic violence came to realize the scope of the problem. We know now that we are not alone in our experiences. We also didn't know that students around us would be so willing to help us with our causes. Rachael and Aaron didn't think they would get any student responses in their school-wide toiletry drive for the homeless; the piles of toothbrushes, shampoo, and soap they were able to collect stunned them.

Through our own projects and those of our peers, we found that we could be selfless. We also came to the realization that our lives could change at any moment; it could be one of our parents who has cancer; it could be one of our siblings who is being abused, our house that burned down. It could be our families' opportunities that are limited because of race or social-economic status. We joined this class for an English credit, but we are leaving inspired to change the world.

Poetry and Power in the Creative Writing Workshop

MAGGIE FOLKERS

After attending a Social Action training session, I began my new school year ready to experiment with the ideas and activities I had learned. My semester-long elective poetry class for eleventh and twelfth graders offered me the freedom to design my own curriculum. The course outline simply states, "This course stresses the belief that all people are poets and anyone can learn how to write as well as read and understand poetry. . . . Through the reading and writing of poetry, students learn that the poetic experience is timeless and universal, and that the poet is an artist." With such a broad description, I could go anywhere, as long as I threaded the state standards of reading, writing, listening, speaking, and researching into the semester.

My decision to restructure the class was based on more than simply the freedom the course offered. I also hoped that the principles and processes of Social Action might transform a sometimes dull, unproductive writers workshop into a place where students made connections, felt inspired, found their voice, wrote with purpose, and felt valued, validated, and motivated to act on issues of concern to them. I longed for students to recognize the fact that their writing had power, influence, and importance and to feel that this wasn't just another activity needed to earn a grade. In retrospect, these were pretty big aspirations.

I began by thinking about how I could establish a new climate in this class, one that would invite students to redefine themselves and work against any oppressive labels. Paolo Freire, in *Pedagogy of the Oppressed,* talks about the fact that liberating and freeing ourselves and others is a process of many steps and can be quite arduous at times (Freire, 1970). What resonates for me from his work is this notion: in order to change a society through education, one must demonstrate a sincere and heartfelt love toward others, remain humble, maintain faith in humankind, possess hope, act on those beliefs, and then reflect on them. He goes on to say that the entire process must begin with dialogue because without communication, there is no education; at the same time, without education, there is no dialogue. This gave me a jumping-off place for the new semester: I would re-design the start of class around dialogue and exploration.

We began with open-ended get-acquainted activities that created the atmosphere of dialogue I had hoped for. From the beginning, students responded positively to classroom conversations that I facilitated rather than directed. Some voiced amazement that I allowed them the freedom to talk, negotiate, draw, create, and interpret in small groups before I even began making assignments and taking grades. I thought about my first-grade son's eagerness to participate in school and his energy for learning and noted similarities to my own classroom: students smiled when they entered and left my room; body language appeared relaxed; unexpected individuals stayed after class to let me know how excited they were to take poetry even though they had not previously liked it. Many looked forward to buying journals and special writing utensils and to using them. I was in shock; after eight semesters of teaching this course, I had fostered a change in attitudes, behaviors, and body language.

As the semester continued, we developed routines and created predictable structures to sustain and channel the work students created for themselves. Each day, poetry class began with twenty minutes of sustained Sacred Writing time for the students and me, followed by sharing. After sharing for ten to twenty minutes, we explored poetic tools, learned strategies for analysis, and read poetry. The class resembled many creative writing workshops in its blend of workshop time, sharing time, and focused study of the craft of writing. I gave students due dates for final drafts in verse, along with rubrics that highlighted the poetic tools we were focusing on for that week, yet I allowed students to choose their own topics because the ones they chose were thoughtful, developed, emotional, and full of voice. I shared my pieces, asked for help with lines and words, provided honest answers when asked questions during group discussions, and simply worked alongside my students.

Something more about this workshop was different, however. In line with the intent of the early stages of Social Action, I encouraged students to write about life experiences, what they did, what they thought, what they liked or did not like about their lives, or whatever was in their heart at the moment. In order for us to refrain from judging others, I facilitated a discussion based on three words: tolerance, acceptance, and approval. We decided that *tolerance* had a negative connotation because it implied we were just going to put up with one another. We concluded that unconditional *acceptance* did not necessarily mean unconditional *approval*. We agreed on the guideline that we would accept people for who they are, but we did not have to approve of their actions.

When students brought up different issues, we followed up with discussions of why those situations existed and what caused problems or concerns in their lives. The students generated topics, responded to issues in journal form, and shared, revised, and edited in small groups. We took time for dialogue, and sometimes debate, as a whole class. These discussions were facilitated but not led by me. Whenever students shared words, phrases, sentences, or ideas, I praised them for their courage and noted their contribution on a tally sheet. Never before had so many students shared aloud just after writing a first draft. What I had discovered was that a poetry class can come alive when writing is connected to issues that matter in the lives of the community.

Contrary to what I had experienced in previous semesters, it was clear that many of my poetry students looked forward to our Sacred Writing and sharing times. They voiced their frustration when assembly schedules or other interruptions shortened it. Of course, not every student shared willingly or enthusiastically right away. A few resisted participating in this decidedly more open atmosphere. However, in time, they began to adhere to the guidelines negotiated and established by their classmates. How on earth did we get to this point? I think the key word is *trust*. Students trusted their peers. Students who were initially skeptical later found themselves supporting and encouraging others verbally or through writing, and looking forward to the validation and feedback that they trusted their peer response group members to provide. It was also crucial that the students trusted me. We worked collectively. The principles of Social Action are designed to bring a group together and recognize that everyone involved is a vital part of that group.

My biggest challenge in facilitating a more democratic classroom involved control. At times, I wanted to ignore the Social Action principles, take charge over every aspect of the classroom, and retreat to formula writing in search of the comfortable, familiar path that had been enforced for most of my life. Definite tensions existed for me while experimenting with this new approach. For one thing, the dialogue, though crucial, took a great amount of time and energy. Lesson plans that I loved never made it out of the filing cabinet. Second, the student dialogue and activities gave the class an unstructured or, to some outsiders, chaotic look that contrasted sharply with the other classes in the building. Finally, I wondered how I should deal with the controversial hot topics and taboo issues the teenagers insisted had relevance, especially when students' views were often antithetical to mine. When we did the Movie Poster activity (see Part Three), student-generated posters that developed into final pieces covered the following topics: the September 11 attacks, AIDS, homophobia, drunk driving, death, racism, ballot issues, gay marriage, movie stars, social segregation in schools, effects of the media and consumerism, security on planes, child poverty and child abuse, terrorism, peer pressure, drug abuse, abortions, anorexia, popularity and the need to fit in, money, sex, the school dress code, the true meaning of punk rock, and severed relationships. Despite my personal beliefs on these issues, I began responding to students' ideas with respect. In return, I found that greater respect developed in the classroom. Students wrote, edited, revised, and published with evident passion because they had found a freedom that many had not experienced earlier in their schooling.

Another difficulty I encountered came from outside the classroom. I shared my experiences with some well-seasoned teachers, hoping to hear some encouraging feedback. Instead, many gave me "the look" and "the lecture," which suggested that my classroom dialogue and writing sessions were inappropriate. After much personal reflection, I decided to shut my door and continue to draw on Social Action principles and practice. I came to the conclusion that I had to allow the class to push content limits, not for the sake of shocking others but because the students had a message. I decided that Social Action was working for my class and that I should see where it would take us, even if I had to look elsewhere for a community of teachers who would support my decision to use Social Action.

The semester's culminating presentation, a poem entitled "Who Am I?" enabled students to consider who they had been in the past, who they were in the present, and where they were headed in the future, as well as what influences had helped shape their lives. An additional requirement of integrating another art form made this work especially challenging. We examined the lives and poems of Jimmy Santiago Baca, Lucille Clifton, Marilyn Chin, David Mura, and Naomi Shihab-Nye, to name a few. We worked on goal setting, listing resources and developing action plans for fulfilling the goals. By the time finals arrived, many students were not ready for class to end. Some hugged and thanked classmates for a productive semester. Tears were shed during their presentations. For the first time, all my students completed their finals. In the past, some had preferred to take a grade deduction instead, as long as they passed and earned credit for the class.

On the day of the final exam, students presented me with a scrapbook full of notes and dedicated poems. One entry came from a senior with whom I had had torturous experiences in a previous class: "Thank you for always making your classroom a place where I always felt safe expressing myself and never giving up on me. . . . Through your class I learned more about myself than I have in the last 4 years. Thank you. You are a great teacher—I am really going to miss you next year." Her final presentation and poem generated applause. Her voice was bold, believable, honest, and backed by a vision.

What a semester! The Social Action principles reinvigorated our class in ways I feel compelled to share with others. I am inspired to train more teachers, so that they too can explore a process that yields results. As of late, I am team-teaching a class of sixty sophomores with a social studies teacher, who at first just went along with suggested activities to accommodate me; now, however, he enthusiastically promotes the activities because we have facilitated some of the most meaningful discussions he has ever encountered. Even more exciting, he has shared the process and activities with his department, which is now considering future training. The news is spreading. I feel encouraged by the potential for collegiality and empowered by the tools offered by Social Action.

Shall We Dance?

CONNIE ELLARD BUNCH

S arah and Matt had attended a school dance over the weekend that was canceled before it even started because of fighting among a few of the students. Even though the great majority of students were well behaved and having fun, administrators wanted to prevent a potentially negative situation. "That's the second time a dance has been shut down 'cause people were fighting," my students explained.

Sarah and Matt are two students in my Intensive Services class for high school juniors and seniors who need anger management skills and positive behavior instruction. The goal of this class, which accommodates one to six students at a time, is to help students develop personal skills that will keep them out of trouble in school. Most of the students in Intensive Services have had behavioral and legal problems in the community and are on probation. Some of them have already been in detention facilities.

We identified the problem: Matt and Sarah had gotten dressed up and had been ready to have fun, only to have a few people ruin the dance for everyone. Now we were ready to find out why the fighting had broken out at the dance. As we delved into the complexity of hot tempers, quick reactions, and intense feelings that shape the world of teenage alliances, I wondered whether these extremely annoyed students would be able to go beyond simple answers. At first, they flung out quick, pat responses to the question of why the fights were occurring. Exploring why the dance had been canceled led to lengthy, at times convoluted, and emotional discussions of the various coalitions and dynamics functioning in their worlds. The students' initial response was that they didn't believe that there was any part of the problem that could be examined by itself in a positive manner. The problem appeared larger than life.

I continued to encourage them to question and brainstorm about the elements of this particular situation instead of analyzing our whole society and global conflicts. We kept coming back to that particular evening and those fifteen minutes that had ruined their plans for the night. As we continued to probe, the students determined that there were two groups responsible for the fights: middle school students and students who had graduated or been expelled. Young people from the second group had come to the dance, even though the event was for currently enrolled high school students only. The uninvited students had used the dance to act out unrelated conflicts.

During their next classes, my students began to brainstorm about how the challenge of uninvited students causing problems at dances could be addressed. How could the troublemakers be kept out, so that the rest of the students could participate in a safe and enjoyable social event? Matt came up with lots of ways to control those who attended, but as we considered the consequences of his ideas, he found that those solutions would only lead to other problems. He analyzed the role of teacher-chaperones who attended the dance as a means of improving the situation but decided that teachers didn't always recognize the students who were not supposed to be at the dance nor the students who were involved in current conflicts in the community.

He continued to think of possible solutions, suggesting, "Maybe a student, like me, could sit where they come in to the dance and keep the troublemakers out." After reflection, Matt and Sarah decided that would not work. If a student kept another student out of the event, there might be hurt feelings or retaliation. Sarah thought that maybe a list of people not allowed inside the dance might be compiled but decided that wouldn't work, either. Students probably wouldn't like it if they found out they were on a list, and it would be difficult to maintain such a list because of the varied behavior and problems at school and in the community.

Exploring these ideas took time and patience on everyone's part but proved worthwhile as Sarah and Matt became focused on the problem in ways that did not involve them personally in the conflict. They were able to find some distance and talk about a concrete event in a less personal way, practicing what we had previously learned about solving problems.

After a time, they thought of an idea they both agreed would work. The school did not have ID cards for the students. If the school started an ID program, the cards could be used to admit the high school students to the dance and keep the younger and older students from entering and possibly causing problems.

As we continued the discussion over the next several days, Matt and Sarah amassed reasons that the ID cards would be useful that went beyond dances, raising the issue of stolen lunch numbers in the cafeteria, for example. "We could use the student ID in the cafeteria, and you would have to have your own ID and maybe put it through a machine, like at the store with a credit card or something. Then nobody could overhear you giving your number for the computerized payment system to the staff person and steal your number and then your lunch."

Matt and Sarah, a pair of kids who had a history of causing problems, being in the middle of trouble situations, and causing conflicts outside of school, continued to think of ways that student IDs could be used positively in the school setting. They suggested that the IDs could be made to look impressive so that students would be proud of them.

I could think of several ways the ID cards could make teachers' jobs easier. ID cards could help us address students whom we didn't have in class and didn't know by name and thus could give us the ability to recognize someone on campus who was not a student at our school. The students went on to suggest that the ID cards could be used to get into sports events and check out library books and that "maybe local businesses would even offer student discounts" when the cards were presented. The ID cards could become a source of pride as well as a means of preventing problems.

But how could Matt and Sarah present their suggestion to the school administration? I suggested that they consider taking their idea to the student government representative. The student government was receptive to the idea of student IDs, and the suggestion is currently being considered by the school administration for the future.

Sarah and Matt came away from the Social Action process with the feeling that they had made a positive impact on their school and on events they cared about. Furthermore, whether or not the school decides to implement the ID procedure, the Social Action approach has enhanced their learning. It complemented other positive behavior techniques that were adapted for the intensive services class. Using the process, Sarah and Matt identified *what* had made them angry; they analyzed *why* the fighting was a problem; then they discussed *how* they could deal with the problem and took the initiative to *act,* suggesting a viable solution to address a real problem in their lives. They experienced the process of problem solving in a peaceful manner, and with this tool for resolving their anger issues through nonviolent means, they gained the ability to transfer these problem-solving steps to other situations in their lives.

The March on John Philip Sousa

ELIZABETH A. DAVIS

Since the population of students in the District of Columbia is predominantly African American, teaching about the civil rights movement is critical in enabling students to better understand and connect past and present issues of discrimination and inequity in their community and the larger society. For many of my students, the decades of the 1950s, 1960s, and 1970s seem distant and disconnected from their lives. The questions and curiosity raised after reading a brief article about their school, John Philip Sousa Middle School, presented more than merely a teachable moment; here was a golden opportunity to connect the civil rights movement to the lives of Sousa's students. The article, just a blurb of a paragraph relegated to the bottom corner of the Metro section of the *Washington Post,* informed readers that John Philip Sousa had been designated a historic landmark by the National Park Service for the role it had played in the desegregation of schools in the District of Columbia.

The school was named after John Philip Sousa, the bandleader. A portrait of Sousa in full regalia hangs in the school's main lobby. Upon entering the school, one sees photographs of every graduating class from 1950 to the present. The students in the photographs, which are arranged chronologically around the lobby walls, change from all white to varying combinations of black and white and, finally, to an all-black student body. Anyone who takes the time to examine the photographs will get a quick study of the racial history of schooling in our nation's capital. For those who listen, the students in the photographs quietly whisper the school's shameful history of denial and racial discrimination.

After I shared the *Washington Post* article with my four technology education classes, my sixth graders asked me, "What is desegregation, and why did it make Sousa Middle School a historic landmark?" My seventh and eighth graders asked, "Does this mean that Sousa will become a museum? When and why was Sousa segregated? What does all this have to do with us right now?" Since I had been unaware that Sousa was one of the schools cited in the famous Supreme Court case *Brown* v. *Board of Education,* I had to conduct my research along with the students. Students searched for information on the Internet, read, discussed, compared, and swapped research findings with one another and with me. The students themselves had identified the "what" step of Social Action. They were discussing issues related to the civil rights movement and their own history.

Although I had perceived this as the perfect teachable moment with built-in connections to my students, I never imagined that this effort would take on a life of its own, continuing to branch in different directions with broader and unexpected civil rights lessons before its completion. I was beginning to truly understand what is meant by "trust the process" within Social Action. While the Social Action process provides steps to follow, facilitators can never know where these steps will take them, and teachers have to be prepared to give up some of their traditional control in the classroom.

READING, WRITING, AND RESEARCHING SOUSA'S HISTORY

The *Bolling* v. *Sharpe* Supreme Court case mentioned in the article led the students backward and forward to other historical moments of the civil rights movement. It led them to *Brown* v. *Board of Education,* then to *Plessy* v. *Ferguson* and to the origins of the "separate but equal" law. Students' curiosity increased as they began to ask parents, teachers, and community members about Spottswood Bolling and Sousa Middle School during the "separate but equal" era. They learned that Spottswood Bolling Jr. was an eleven-year-old African American boy who had walked in the front door and asked to be enrolled in what was then a brand-new, state-of-the-art facility on the white side of the District of Columbia's legally segregated school system. When the principal refused, Spottswood's mother sued.

When one student described the story as "separate but not equal," I knew that he understood the larger implications of the case and would be able to make connections to more current issues of inequity. At this point, I knew that the students were embarking on the "why" step of Social Action; they wanted to research why these issues existed in their own history and what they meant for their present and future.

I used a variety of texts to further expose students to these issues. While enhancing literacy was one of the underlying goals of the project, critical literacy became one of the more ambitious objectives. My desire was for them not only to read the lines of the text they discovered but also to read between the lines. I wanted them to answer questions about what they had read while critically examining the text and questioning its validity. As a teacher committed to social justice and still learning how to work through the Social Action process, I believed that this questioning and inquiry would prove to be one of the most valuable lessons my students would gain from this project.

Since I continued to be only about a quarter of a step ahead of them in their inquiry, I became the "guide on the side" rather than the "sage on the stage." I mastered the art of answering their questions with more questions. Although it was unsettling at first, I soon began to embrace the notion that this simultaneous, collaborative pedagogy could become the practice for the duration of (what I perceived to be at the time) a unit of study. Each piece of research generated new questions and deeper inquiry. I happily joined the community of learners as a student and co-collaborator rather than the teacher. In the language of Social Action, I was embracing the role of facilitator and becoming accustomed to giving up some of my traditional control.

PARENTS, PARTNERS, AND OTHER COLLABORATORS

Students, teachers, parents, and community members collaborated to identify people from the community who could express what it was like to grow up during the era of segregation. The PTA president contacted William Wilson, a community representative who had attended school with Spottswood Bolling. Wilson, a public school advocate and an icon in the Marshall Heights community, agreed to talk to my students about some of his school and personal experiences as a black youth growing up in the era of "separate but equal."

Students were shocked and impressed by Wilson's experience and by the fact that not only had he been a classmate of Spottswood Bolling but he was still living in the neighborhood. He shared intricate details about how he had walked more than thirty blocks to and from all-black Shaw Junior High School each day, although Sousa was right across the street from where he lived. His firsthand account was the story behind the story of Spottswood Bolling. Wilson became history that day, his account carrying more validity than all of the articles pulled from the World Wide Web. Students had so many questions that, at their request, Wilson came back to serve as a primary source throughout our study.

MAKING THE CASE TO SAVE SOUSA

On one of his return visits, Wilson informed students that the District of Columbia Public Schools' board of education had voted to allocate $14 million to demolish Sousa Middle School and build a new school on the site. He explained that as a result, Sousa Middle School would lose its status as a historic landmark. After much discussion about the pros and cons of razing versus renovation of the school and the significance of preserving one's history, the students agreed that the history of the school was too important to them and to the community to be destroyed. They knew that they had to make their case for saving the school's designation as a historic landmark to the school board, the city council, and the community. In his letter to the board, eighth grader Kirk Washington wrote that he wanted to preserve the school building "because I am an African-American and Sousa is an important part of my history."

So began a student-led campaign to save John Philip Sousa Middle School. In accordance with the Social Action process, students had identified one part of "how" they were going to save their school—educating the community about the school's status as a historic landmark. With that decided, researching, reading, writing, and resisting became the order of the day. I was thrilled that this project not only raised consciousness about the civil rights movement and school history but also increased student awareness of the power of the pen and the need to be able to express ideas through the written word.

The "act" step of Social Action manifested itself in many different ways as students took various actions to save their school as a historic landmark while educating the whole community about their history. Some students wrote articles for a special classroom publication called *Uprisings*. Letters were sent to key board and council members, and a petition was drafted to support the renovation of Sousa. Several teams from each class volunteered to plan "Spotlight on Spottswood Bolling

Day," a day planned by students and approved by the principal. During the day, teams of four students were dispatched to each homeroom to conduct orientations about the *Bolling* v. *Sharpe* case and to make the case for saving the school as a historic landmark. In my class, the teams debriefed and critiqued their performance delivery and knowledge of the subject. In addition, they used audience evaluations. This feedback represented the "reflect" step of the process, and many students felt a great sense of accomplishment as a result of it.

The universal willingness of students, teachers, support staff, and parents to sign the petition to save the school was an indication that the campaign was working. Students were beginning to realize their own power. They now had the confidence and motivation to continue.

DESIGNING STUDENTS REDESIGN JOHN PHILIP SOUSA

Although the architectural planning committee and the board favored the least expensive option—razing Sousa to build a new school—they were obligated to seek community input before doing so. Neither the board nor the architectural planning committee anticipated authentic student, parent, and community engagement with Sousa's capital improvement plan. Several students attended the architectural planning team's community meetings. They noted that other than Wilson, there were few people fighting to preserve the school as a historic landmark. Traditionally, parents in this low-income African American community have not been valued as informed decision makers, nor have they been engaged in policy decisions made in or about the school. In general, civic engagement is negatively affected by the District of Columbia's lack of Congressional representation and the failure of local school leaders in predominantly low-income communities of color to cultivate participatory decision making with informed and engaged parents. Discrimination based on race and class continues to thrive in a city that is noted for the role it played in the racial desegregation of public schools in our nation.

The ninety-eight students working on the campaign to save the school decided to create their own vision of a renovated school. They learned from Wilson that "compromising the integrity of the structure" in any way would result in the school losing its designation as a historic landmark. The structure had to be saved, not destroyed. As a prologue to the letter-writing campaign, drive for petition signatures, and schoolwide orientations, they began constructing a scale model of their vision for the renovated John Philip Sousa. Each student chose an area of the school to redesign, and Christina Hayunga, a volunteer architect, came to the school once a week for two months to advise them.

THE VICTORY

As they continued their investigation of the Spottswood Bolling story, the students were ecstatic to learn that the board of education had decided to allocate an additional $4 million for the renovation of John Philip Sousa. They were equally excited about the critical role they had played in the continuing legacy of Spottswood Bolling. As they continued to reflect on the process, students realized that they had gained a restored, state-of-the-art, twenty-first-century school while preserving Sousa's status as a National Historic Landmark. They had learned that collective actions have the power to achieve a goal and that the civil rights movement was not merely one event orchestrated by one or a few people but a series of events and actions collaboratively and strategically planned and carried out by many to achieve equity and justice for all. More important, students began to understand how they continue to benefit from events that occurred over a century ago to secure civil and human rights for people of color. The research project helped them to see that the civil rights movement is not an era that has ended but an ongoing struggle that will require their engagement as responsible citizens who seek to secure and maintain a just society.

Did the project enable students to draw parallels between the events that led to the Brown, Bolling, and Plessy cases and current social injustices stemming from racial, cultural, and socioeconomic differences in their school and community? Will they now be able to identify examples of discriminatory practices embedded in some of the policy decisions made in and about their own school, school district, and community at large? I would answer "yes" to each of these questions. As a result of the project, the civil rights movement became more than just a page of history for these students; it became a meaningful part of their lives. This was evidenced in their desire to pursue further research about the school's history and in their desire to preserve it for future generations. It was also evidenced in their willingness to take on this task and follow through with all of the work needed to complete it. Without necessarily realizing it, the students propelled themselves through the steps of Social Action while I facilitated along the way.

Social Action and Parent Involvement

MILDRED SERRA

For nine years, I have worked at the Francisco Felicie Martinez School in Breñas, Vega Alta. The school lies on the northern coast of Puerto Rico in an area separated from the Atlantic Ocean by a busy highway. Although the school is presently bordered by retirement condominiums, many of the students come from a community of squatters near the school. The residents of these areas deal with the lack of public utilities and constant threat of eviction.

Despite the challenges that the community faces, my school is well-run and supportive of the young people who attend. Despite our efforts to create a welcoming atmosphere, however, teachers and students have been concerned about a seeming lack of parent involvement. Students in our school have repeatedly expressed that they would like to see their parents participate in school activities and work as volunteers. They have also mentioned that they are frustrated with the lack of attention that they receive at home; for instance, many would like help from their parents with homework. I knew we'd be able to serve our students better if their parents got involved, yet the challenges that parents face as they work to support their families in our community make involvement with their children's schooling difficult. I wondered whether using Social Action to get parents more involved in the school would be a positive step.

I had the idea that my colleagues and I could create workshops based on Social Action principles for the local parents. After the director of our school agreed to this, I invited teacher colleagues from the Borinquen Writing Project who had participated in Social Action workshops to work with me. I wanted these workshops to do two things: to train parents in Social Action strategies and to take three teachers through the process of training the parents so that we could support each other and learn from the experience.

My school director and I sent letters inviting parents to apply for these workshops and offering a stipend. We received thirty applications, a large number, and wondered whether the stipend was part of the draw. We asked each applicant to write—or speak, if they could not write—a short explanation of why they wanted to take part. While some wrote "por el dinero" (for the money), most expressed a desire to help their children. Although we originally had had funds for only fifteen parents, we secured support to accommodate twenty.

All of the participants were women, though as the workshops continued, their husbands occasionally showed up. Many of the parents who participated had students in special education and in their applications expressed worry about whether their children's needs were being met by the school. Some felt that they could not advocate for their children. Sixteen of the twenty participants lived in Villa Alegre, a squatters' community on government property. As they described their community, we learned that there is no sewage system or garbage pickup at Villa Alegre; residents live in makeshift houses, some without running water and some with gas generators to provide electricity. When I first visited the community, I was told by one of my students to stay near the road because some of the residents use the more remote parts of the area to store stolen horses and cars.

Parents arrived at the first session with apparent misgivings. Some were hesitant to enter the school library, where the workshops were held, and many were reluctant to speak. At this meeting, we used a range of icebreakers to start the long process of building community and helping parents feel comfortable in the school setting. We distributed an agenda for the day, discussed the best schedule for the workshops, and gave the participants an opportunity to share what was on their minds. We also provided a "welcome" snack. By the end of the first meeting, the parents were more relaxed.

One of the major challenges we faced as facilitators was convincing the parents that teachers valued their opinions. We used different strategies to help the parents feel comfortable and to help them understand that we respected their input and experience. We chose game-like activities that defused tension, and we focused on what parents had to say about their lives. In one activity called "The Treasure I

See," a teacher told the parents that she wanted them to come up and look in a small chest and then, without speaking, return to their seats and write or draw what was valuable about the treasure. The first person came forward and laughed when she looked in the box. Then she walked back to her seat and began to write. When the next participant came forward, she too laughed: the box contained a mirror. The mothers grew closer through their enjoyment of the activity and were eager to open up more.

In an activity called "Hot Seat," only the individual sitting in the center of the room in the hot seat could speak. This person would describe a problem, and those who wanted either to offer solutions or to get information had to sit in the hot seat in order to speak. Participants in this activity were able to hold the group's attention and speak uninterrupted. During this time, they identified problems such as providing necessities for their children, heavy drinking among the community's fathers, and an issue that they later worked on: the trash piling up on the land where they lived.

In addition to our choice of activities, we also encouraged the participants to express themselves in a variety of ways, including drawing, miming, and speaking. Many of the women felt more comfortable using sign systems other than writing, but once they were more comfortable with the training sessions, they also began to write. By the end of the sixth workshop, their notebooks were full. My colleagues and I reflected on the time and effort we had invested in allowing the parents to form a group, become relaxed and expressive, and come to trust us as facilitators, despite their feelings about teachers. We noted how rare it is for parent involvement efforts to make this investment.

After their initial reserve, parents became eager for our Tuesday and Thursday meetings to arrive. Sometimes their children would come along, though I hadn't planned on their attendance. These young people became valuable participants, however, helping to serve snacks and working with their parents during activities. One of the students who attended said that she had never had the opportunity to do anything like this with her mother until then.

Once we were ready to talk about specific issues that the group might address, we divided into smaller groups and used different activities, including But Why? (see Part Three) to identify problems—which were overabundant. Groups wrote their lists of issues and posted them on the walls. Other groups then walked around, writing down possible solutions next to the problems. These parents, many of whom had felt helpless and had often waited for others to come and solve their problems, were beginning to identify their own solutions.

The workshops ended around Christmastime, and we could not hold a follow-up meeting until April. When the group gathered again, we were surprised by what we heard. Six of the women showed up and began to talk about how things had changed for the participants. Many of the women were not at the meeting because they had gotten jobs. Others had begun to look for jobs, and one of the participants was volunteering at the school. As a group, these parents now knew more about the school and had met and spoken with the principal. They talked about becoming advocates for their children. One of the daughters came to the session and expressed pride that her mother was meeting with parents and teachers.

Things changed even more over the course of the next year. The women of Villa Alegre who had participated in the workshops wrote a letter to the mayor complaining about the lack of garbage removal in their area, and the town responded by sending garbage trucks. The garbage pickup was orderly and successful because these same women had organized the community to collect the garbage in one place at an appointed time. The group also requested that the school provide after-school activities, and the principal responded by turning the building into an "open school" with activities from 3:00 to 5:30 P.M. every day. The involvement of many of these parents in the school community continues to this day.

What explains these changes? I believe that the parents who participated in the Social Action workshop have come to see that if they work together, they can change things both in the school and at home. Many attempts to build parent involvement at schools start with what the school wants from the parents. In Social Action, we started with determining what parents wanted for themselves and helping them work to achieve it for themselves. That became a lesson that continued for them—and for us—long after the workshops ended.

APPENDIX

Following is a Spanish translation of the Social Action Process and Principles prepared by Mark Wekander, former director, and Crucita Orama, former co-director of the Borinquen Writing Project in Puerto Rico. This translation has been used to facilitate Social Action training with Spanish-speaking teachers and parents at the Borinquen site.

Etapas en el Proceso de Acción Social

El papel del facilitador de la Acción Social es asistir al grupo a pasar por las cinco etapas del proceso. No es proveer las soluciones a la gente o hacer las cosas por ellos. El proceso de tomar decisiones pertenece a los miembros de la comunidad y el facilitador o la facilitadora trabaja en conjunto con ellos.

Qué. Los miembros del grupo comparten sus experiencias de la vida: lo que hacen, lo que piensan, lo que les gusta y no les gusta de sus vidas, y etc. Las decisiones del grupo formarán la imagen de lo que ellos quieren, creada por una variedad de medios, como la discusión, el video, la fotografía, cuentos, etc.

Por Qué. ¿Por qué existen estas situaciones? ¿Cuáles son las causas de estos problemas y preocupaciones? La meta de esta etapa es capacitar a la gente, quien no ha tenido la oportunidad hasta ahora, para presentar cómo ellos entienden sus propias situaciones. Esta etapa contradice el concepto tradicional que solamente los profesionales entrenados pueden identificar los problemas y llegar a soluciones.

Cómo. ¿Cómo se puede cambiar la situación? ¿Qué podemos hacer para cambiar la situación? La responsabilidad del facilitador en esta etapa es capacitar al grupo para probar sus propias teorías y conclusiones en un ambiente más seguro adentro del grupo que él del mundo exterior. El o ella necesitará manejar las expectativas del grupo y ayudará para que pueda mantener metas realistas sin mermar el entusiasmo del grupo.

Acción. Cualquier acción que ponga en práctica el grupo no necesariamente ofrecerá una solución a los problemas existentes, pero el producto del intento será una herramienta que se pueda usar para solucionar los problemas y sentirse capacitado.

Reflexión. La oportunidad para la reflexión crítica en la fase de acción capacita a los participantes para planificar nuevas acciones y cambios, utilizando el proceso de Qué, Por qué, Cómo, Acción Social otra vez.

Los Principios de Acción Social

- Los principios de la Acción Social resumen las creencias sobre las destrezas no reconocidas y las capacidades de la gente marginada por la comunidad general y afirma el derecho de los grupos marginados a determinar sus propios futuros, el poder del trabajo colectivo y los principios éticos que deben mostrar los profesionales quiénes trabajan con estos grupos.

   Los trabajadores de la Acción Social tienen un compromiso con la justicia social. Luchamos en contra de la inequidad y la opresión con relación a la raza, el género, la sexualidad, la vejez, la religión, las clases sociales, cultura, impedimentos, o cualquier forma de diferencia social.

- Creemos que todos tienen destrezas, experiencias, y entendimiento que los pueden utilizar para trabajar con los problemas que enfrentan. Los trabajadores de la Acción Social entienden que las personas son expertas en las condiciones de sus propias vidas y utilizamos su conocimiento como el punto para empezar nuestro trabajo.

- Todos tienen derechos, entre los cuales se incluye el derecho a ser escuchados, el derecho a definir los asuntos que se enfrentan y el derecho a iniciar acciones por el beneficio de sus propias vidas. La gente también tiene el derecho a definir quiénes son y no ser estigmatizados por nombres negativos impuestos por otros.

- La injusticia y la opresión son asuntos complejos relacionados a la política social, el ambiente y la economía. Los trabajadores de la Acción Social entienden que la gente vive los problemas como individuos pero que estas dificultades pueden ser vistas como preocupaciones comunes. Entendemos que la colaboración de la gente puede ser muy poderosa. La gente que no tiene poder ni influencia para enfrentar la injusticia y la opresión, los pueden adquirir mediante la colaboración con personas en una situación similar.

- Los trabajadores de la Acción Social no son líderes, pero son facilitadores. El trabajo de nosotros es adiestra a la gente para que ella pueda tomar sus propias decisiones y reclamar como suyos los resultados de sus acciones, no importa los resultados. Las contribuciones de todos son de igual valor y es muy importante que el trabajo de noso.

PART TWO

Getting Started
with Social Action

How exactly does Social Action fit into a classroom? With its emphasis on the
fundamental value of student contribution and professional growth, Social
Action practice embodies ideas that resonate with many teachers. While the teachers involved in the collaboration understood these ideas, they weren't entirely prepared for how much their role in the classroom would change and how much their
own students would change as they worked toward change in their lives. Chapter
Twelve explores the tensions, benefits, and complexities of the work and provides
a more in-depth grounding in the theory behind the Social Action principles and
practice as it was developed over time by the Centre for Social Action. Chapter
Thirteen presents the theory and practice behind Social Action. Chapter Fourteen
sets out some things to think about before you start to introduce Social Action into
your classroom.

Learning from Social Action

Reflections on Teaching and Social Action

When National Writing Project teachers first began learning about Social Action, they came to the process with a passion for teaching and a commitment to student-centered learning, but they also had some doubts about whether Social Action could work in the classroom. Teachers are responsible for setting the agenda for learning each day as well as covering curricular material in order to meet standards. How can Social Action be incorporated into the day-to-day routines of a classroom when the process itself asks the teacher to facilitate rather than lead? How does it affect a teacher's accountability and authority to allow the students to determine some of the content and even the direction of their own learning?

Once NWP teachers had an opportunity to think deeply together about the principles and process of Social Action, they realized there were compelling intersections with their own teaching practice that merited further consideration. The teachers' own experiences resonated with the ideas that students should have an investment in their own learning, that students benefit from opportunities to lead as well as be good group members, and that developing critical thinking and literacy skills can help to ensure a better future for students as they become adults in their larger communities.

The stories included in this book not only highlight the innovative possibilities of Social Action but also serve as examples of how teachers successfully adapted the process and philosophy while working within existing structures.

Teachers modified classroom routines and created out-of-the-ordinary lessons as they used their Social Action training to work with students. In the process of doing so, they discovered that their students, including their struggling learners, became more engaged and motivated to learn. They also discovered that rather than distracting from the standard curriculum, Social Action provided a real context for developing students' literacy skills. At several points during the NWP-CSA collaboration, teachers met to analyze these ideas and experiences, distilling three key ideas: teachable moments as critical opportunities; the power of Social Action to engage and motivate students; and teachers as facilitators in the Social Action classroom.

TEACHABLE MOMENTS AS CRITICAL OPPORTUNITIES

Social Action, which encourages creative practice in student-centered environments, can start as a response to a "teachable moment," capitalizing on an opportunity to connect schooling and curriculum to student lives. NWP teachers who were trained in the Social Action principles and process were initially daunted by the prospect of bringing it back to their classroom. The very words *Social Action* brought to mind a huge project that would take over the classroom, leaving teachers little or no time for the subject areas they were responsible for covering each year. In practice, however, Social Action was much more flexible than it had appeared at first. Many of the teachers featured in this book didn't necessarily plan in advance to use Social Action in their classroom but used the process as a framework to build on a serendipitous teachable moment.

An example of such capitalization on a teachable moment is offered by Elizabeth Davis in Chapter Ten. What began as simply reading an article with her students about the history of their school turned into an opportunity to look deeply at a much larger issue in the community. Davis expressed it this way: "Although I had perceived this as the perfect teachable moment with built-in connections to my students, I never imagined that this effort would take on a life of its own, continuing to branch in different directions with broader and unexpected civil rights lessons before its completion." Working within the framework of Social Action allowed Davis and her students to enhance learning that was already taking place in the classroom, to engage as co-learners in a critical literacy inquiry, and then go on to make change in their larger community.

The range of teacher stories illustrates the adaptability of Social Action to groups of varying sizes with varying goals. As evidenced by the Youth Dreamers, given the right circumstances, Social Action can have tremendous outcomes for the group. But while the Youth Dreamers' project constitutes Social Action on a grand scale, it is important to note that each teacher writing in this book used Social Action in a way that worked for her. Paula Laub (Chapter Two) used the process with her first graders to initiate smaller but no less significant changes within their school. Social Action helped Lori Farias facilitate her students' taking greater control of their choices for service learning, a requirement of her elective high school English course (see Chapter Seven). In each of these examples, students began to see themselves as having a voice with power to make real change, and teachers had an opportunity to reflect on classroom practice in productive ways. The Social Action process provided possibilities for both finding and responding to teachable moments and enabled teachers to revise more typical approaches to curriculum and social or behavioral issues.

THE POWER OF SOCIAL ACTION TO ENGAGE AND MOTIVATE STUDENTS

Teachers are accustomed to setting the agenda for learning in the classroom each day and guiding students productively through lesson plans, so the idea of allowing students to direct the learning agenda at first seemed overwhelming and impractical, if not impossible. If a Social Action approach were applied in the classroom, teachers wondered, would students still choose to engage in the learning process, or would the classroom environment become chaotic and unmanageable? Even though these teachers believed in the Social Action principles and process, they were skeptical about whether it could really work. Yet the teachers who went on to use Social Action in their classrooms found that working with students in the process in fact helped students acquire skills that stretched far beyond English and language arts to other disciplines.

Maggie Folker's decision to use Social Action in an elective poetry class (Chapter Eight) improved the perceptions of the students not only toward the subject matter but also toward each other, the teacher, and the school itself. Her use of Social Action activities with the class created a participative environment, which she capitalized on to facilitate critical reflection in her students. Elizabeth Davis and her students at Sousa Middle School conducted research together and compared their findings, discussing the validity of the texts and reflecting on the larger implications for themselves as community members (see Chapter Ten). As these examples clearly show, Social Action can be adapted to energize curriculum that students may have previously found unrelated to the context of their lives. Far from taking class time away from literacy activities, Social Action in practice created a real context that catalyzed academic learning.

Using Social Action invites young people to shape the learning process by encouraging them to share their thoughts, beliefs, and experiences as core content in the classroom. This is not to suggest that the process does not present challenges. In Chapter Three, Dietta Hitchcock learns that asking students what they think demands a willingness on the teacher's part to hear "the kinds of truths that are most difficult to accept" rather than assuming that students share the teacher's concerns. But engaging with her students on these difficult truths was a valuable experience for her as a professional, and her classroom benefited from increased student motivation and participation as a result.

The Social Action approach is successful not only with students who excel in academic settings, but perhaps even more so with students who may be marginalized in the school community, such as struggling learners or English language learners. Consider Kristina Berdan's student who was failing all of her other classes but was the leader in the Youth Dreamers (Chapter Five). Or Connie Bunch, who, rather than managing or controlling student behavior, recognized that two students who were often perceived as troublemakers were experts in the situation and that the Social Action process could help them use their knowledge to come up with solutions to their problem (Chapter Nine).

The Social Action process was originally conceived to work with young people who had been excluded from or felt marginalized in academic settings. Its origins may account for the way that it can facilitate meaningful connections in the community outside of the classroom as well as inside of it. Chapter Eleven dramatically showcases the possibilities for working with different groups of people. Parents' participation in the Social Action workshops planted the seed for change to take place in their communities even after the workshops were over.

TEACHERS AS FACILITATORS IN THE SOCIAL ACTION CLASSROOM

While the teachers in this book believe that their students participated in richer experiences as a result of their choice to use elements of Social Action, they often struggled with their role as teacher versus their role as facilitator. The teachers were still responsible for education and discipline in their classrooms; they were still accountable to administrators and parents; and they were still expected to be the authority in terms of content of the curriculum, standards, and assessment. Yet they were able to trust the Social Action process, give up some of the control that they had traditionally assumed, and fit Social Action principles into the classroom. Sometimes institutional limitations of time, standard curricula, testing, and daily interruptions place constraints on how Social Action can be used in the classroom. The teachers in this volume were able to work around those constraints.

While some teachers feel it is impossible for Social Action to work in a pure sense in the classroom because of the power imbalances between a teacher and students, these teachers felt that there was scope within the classroom for Social Action to be offered and for teachers to be facilitators rather than leaders. Having to decide when to relinquish control over the students and the subject matter creates tensions for teachers that can be both rewarding and frustrating, especially when the teacher must let go and let the group control the outcomes of the Social Action process. But it was through this kind of collaboration that the teachers were able to broaden students' opportunities to use language and increase their skills in real and meaningful contexts within their own lives.

Another aspect of accountability for teachers to consider is that using Social Action demands responsibility to the students themselves. This concept is familiar to teachers, but in a Social Action context, a teacher-facilitator can't stop in the middle of the process or choose not to follow through on at least some of the ideas presented by the group. Perhaps the most striking example of this tension is the story of the Youth Dreamers and their teacher, Kristina Berdan (Chapter Five). Given a project of that scale, there have been moments when Berdan considered giving up. She reflects that the project has taken over her life to a large extent; the work has been rewarding but also exhausting. The many references by teachers in this book to a Social Action project taking on a life of its own and the unpredictability of the outcomes represent real challenges for teachers; however, the times when teachers let Social Action take on its own life were when the most creative and exciting work was done by the young people.

WRITING FOR A CHANGE

Despite the complexities and challenges involved, Social Action can work in the classroom; as shown in these stories, it can reinvigorate the relationship between students and teachers, help students gain ownership of their education, and broaden the classroom horizon. Social Action, building on the ideas of Paolo Freire, is about education and learning; learning happened when teachers relinquished their traditional roles and trusted their students and the Social Action process.

Social Action isn't about participants always getting what they want, but about learning to use the process so that all involved know they have a stake in the decisions made. Taken as a whole, these teachers' stories show that the process can be transformative for both youths and adults. Social Action practice allows the participants to see themselves as agents of change and as stakeholders in their own communities. Whether used with first graders, middle school students, or parents, Social Action has the potential to initiate change and fundamentally alter how groups perceive themselves within the context of their larger community. As Paula Laub tested out the Social Action process with her first graders (Chapter Two), she realized that "at six and seven years of age, these students already believed they were powerless to make change." Reflecting on the implications of her experiments with the process, she writes, "What is really encouraging to me is how my students are now so much more at ease with thinking of themselves as agents of change." Social Action can provide an all-too-rare occasion for students and teachers alike to realize that their words and thoughts can matter.

Principles for Practice
What is Social Action?

JENNIE FLEMING, IAN BOULTON

This chapter describes how Social Action is different from the commonly understood concept of social action, covering the principles and theory behind Social Action and the process for conducting Social Action activities in the community and classroom.

Social Action is a community development theory based on the simple premise that *change is possible*. The Social Action approach enables groups of all ages and circumstances to take action and to achieve their collective goals. It offers an easy-to-understand, open-ended process that enables people to identify and act on issues that are important to them while working within a set of principles. For us at the Centre for Social Action, Social Action is a distinctive methodology and should not be confused with the generic term *social action*, which describes activity aimed at bringing about change in society.

Social Action redefines the relationship between professionals and service users—in this case, between teachers and young people. It presents a democratic framework for true partnership, and it is inclusive rather than exclusive. Social Action has the potential to engage the most hard-to-reach young people because it starts from their understanding of what needs to change and relies on their efforts to change it. This approach contrasts with many others that define young people as the problem to be tackled or changed. Social Action views young people, parents, and communities as experts about their lives and as capable of creating positive and lasting social change.

WHAT IS DIFFERENT ABOUT SOCIAL ACTION?

Social Action differs from traditional pedagogy in three important aspects:

- Young people set the agenda.
- Social Action workers and group members work in partnership.
- All people are viewed as having the capacity to create social change and are given the opportunity to do so.

Social Action draws heavily on the work of the Brazilian educator Paolo Freire, who linked literacy with social change. In *Pedagogy of the Oppressed* (Freire, 1970) he describes traditional education as the "banking approach" (Hope and Timmel, 1999, p. 19). In this setting, the student is treated as an empty vessel into which the teacher pours knowledge. Social Action draws on Freire's ideas to suggest a problem-posing approach to education.

SOCIAL ACTION PRINCIPLES

Social Action combines two essential and inseparable elements: principles and process. These are completely dependent on each other. The principles elevate the process beyond a set of techniques that are barely distinguishable from other practices (see Figure 13.1). Similarly, the principles without the process are unlikely to foster action or change.

Social Action is continually developing and changing as a way of working. The changes take place within a framework of values, principles, and processes that evolve over time and change in detail but are nonnegotiable in terms of their over-arching view of the world.

THE SOCIAL ACTION PROCESS

The process is meant to ensure that the relationship between young people (or other service users) and the professionals employed to work with them is equitable. A Social Action worker is a facilitator, not a provider, and his or her role is to facilitate the group through a five-stage process (see Figure 13.2).

The five stages of Social Action are as follows:

What. This stage is about discovery. The goal is to find out what is happening in people's lives. What are their issues, problems, and concerns? What makes them

Figure 13.1. The Social Action Principles

The principles that guide the work of the Centre for Social Action are as follows:

- *Social Action workers are committed to social justice. We strive to challenge inequality and oppression as a result of race, gender, sexuality, age, religion, class, disability, or any other form of social differentiation.* Social Action is about fighting for equality and justice, and this needs to be stated clearly at the beginning of any training, workshop, or class that is using the process. We recognize that injustice, discrimination, and oppression exist and take a stance against them in all our work.
- *We believe that all people have skills, experience, and understanding that they can draw on to tackle the problems they face. Social Action workers understand that people are experts in their own lives, and we use this as a starting point for our work.* Our job is to help uncover what is already there, to encourage people to use the insights and knowledge they possess to bring about changes in their own lives.
- *All people have rights, including the right to be heard, the right to define the issues facing them, and the right to take action on their own behalf. People also have the right to define themselves and not have negative labels imposed on them.* Ordinary people's right to be involved in the changes that affect them, to have a voice and a stake in the society they live in, is fundamental to Social Action work. People's right to "name their world"—to define themselves and the world around them—is something we insist on. Too often, people have to contend with labels imposed on them or the places they live for the case of policymakers and professionals.
- *Injustice and oppression are complex issues rooted in social policy, the environment, and the economy. Social Action workers understand that people may experience problems as individuals but that these difficulties can be translated into common concerns.* We recognize that there are many different problems in individuals' lives. They may feel overwhelmed and daunted by them; they may even feel responsible for them. Social Action gives people the opportunity to break free from this negative view,

Continued

to understand their individual problems in a wider political context, and to do something about organizing to overcome them.

- *We understand that people working collectively can be powerful. People who lack the power and influence to challenge injustice and oppression as individuals can gain it through working with other people in a similar position.* Oppression is experienced by a majority of people; thus, it can only be maintained through isolation and division. Our job is to bring people together so that they can share their experiences and pool their resources and skills to fight injustice. Finding common cause may give individuals the will and power to tackle more complex issues than they might have dared on their own.

- *Social Action workers are not leaders, but facilitators. Our job is to enable people to make decisions for themselves and to take ownership of whatever outcome ensues. Everybody's contribution to this process is equally valued, and it is vital that our job not be accorded privilege.* Social Action workers value all skills and knowledge equally, making no distinction between experience and formal qualifications. Our job is to work alongside the group, resisting the temptation to become either a group member or a group leader.

angry, frightened, happy, and frustrated? What occupies their thoughts? The Social Action worker designs ways in which community members can express this, creating as comprehensive a picture as possible of what is going on in their lives at present, *without interpretation* and without having to worry about what to do with the material. This is often the longest stage of the Social Action process. Video, role-playing, photography, drawing, and discussion may be used during this exploration of life in the community.

Why. Once the issues have been agreed on, it is important to identify the reasons why they exist so that any solutions devised will attack root causes, not just symptoms. Asking "why?" helps people examine their private troubles in a wider context. It provides them with a deeper understanding of the causes, which is necessary if community members and service users are to go on to create and own positive social change. This stage of the process allows community members to engage in analysis and to present their understanding of the problems facing them. This stage

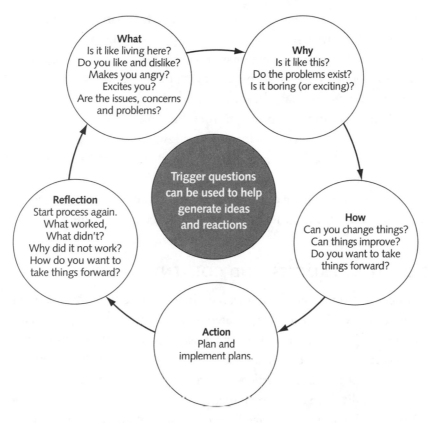

Figure 13.2. The Social Action Process

Source: Centre for Social Action and the Guinness Trust, 2000, p. 10.

also helps participants to discover the most effective point of intervention, the place at which it is possible to make changes that will affect the final outcomes. This analysis is accepted by the Social Action worker, again, without interpretation, reinforcing one of our basic beliefs: people are experts on their own lives.

How. So what do we do with this understanding? How can people change things in a meaningful way? Here the role of the Social Action worker changes. The facilitator's responsibility now is to create safe spaces where the group can test out their ideas for change before putting them into practice. It is vital that community members not be set up to fail and that their ideas undergo rigorous examination before they take them into the world outside the group. The decision about which ideas will be taken forward lies in the hands of the group; the Social Action worker must question their viability without crushing enthusiasm.

Action. Next, the group members put their ideas for change into effect. By now, the group should have a realistic sense of the possible outcomes, whether these outcomes will solve their problem or simply be the first stage in a longer struggle. Even if the action disappoints, as sometimes happens, the legacy of the work is that the group members now have an understanding and practical experience of the tools needed for dealing with problems that they will face in the future.

Reflection. The fifth stage calls for the Social Action worker to bring the group together and ask "What happened? Now that we have carried out our action, are your issues, problems, and concerns the same?" This critical reflection enables community members to learn from their experience and to plan future actions for change. The What? Why? How? process, which is recursive, begins again.

FACILITATION, PROCESS, AND CONTENT

Using Social Action in the classroom redefines the role of the professional away from that of leader. The role is negotiated with the input of the group. This is not about diminishing the importance of professionals such as teachers. Being a good teacher-facilitator requires a great deal of skill and discipline and a combination of diverse skills. Using Social Action requires thorough preparation, active listening, and the ability to be creative, patient, disciplined, and interested in people's lives. The Social Action teacher-facilitator must also maintain a consistent, realistic level of optimistic energy that will fire the group. All of these are qualities of effective teaching practice as well.

When a teacher-facilitator uses the Social Action process in the classroom, students are not just consumers but active agents for change. This can be a difficult balance for some teachers to achieve. For others, as illustrated by some of the stories in this volume, it is liberating.

Social Action facilitation is a discipline with its own particular qualities. The teacher-facilitator helps participants—students, parents, or colleagues—identify which issues they wish to address. The Social Action worker provides a safe environment in which these issues can be explored and poses the most effective questions to the group in the most effective way. As shown in Figure 13.3, a Social Action worker provides the process for a group's Social Action project. The line in the diagram is one that the Social Action worker does not cross; a Social Action worker is restricted to being responsible for the process rather than providing the content.

Social Action worker	Community members or students
What	are the issues, concerns, and problems that the group faces?
Why	do they exist?
How	can they be changed?
Action	Do it!
Reflection	Review what has happened, what has changed, and what still needs to be done, then start the process again.

Figure 13.3. Responsibilities of the Social Action Worker and Group Members

Professionals often make ill-informed or inaccurate assumptions about people's lives. In contrast, effective Social Action workers ask searching questions that enable people to fully explore what is going on in their lives. To say that young people or other group members provide content means that they share their ideas, beliefs, and experiences. They must identify the issues at the center of the work and provide the analysis, action plans, action, and critical reflection. A Social Action worker should support, work alongside, and encourage but not take over. This may be a different way of working for many teachers, all of whom are paid for what they know and for their input into group learning and discussions. In order to be effective Social Action workers, teachers need to go through a process of developing additional facilitation skills that allow the students to fill in the silences. Not only does this process help to achieve desired changes through Social Action, but in its reliance on discovery learning and peer education, it links teaching and learning.

A teacher-facilitator must understand the stages of Social Action and keep the group on track. The process should be explained at the outset and should be well understood by the group. A teacher-facilitator using Social Action must also know where a group is in the process and when to move on. Of course, every Social Action group is different; Group B may do three stages in one lesson, while Group A may take three months on one phase. Similarly, process-led work often means allowing groups to take what may seem like a tortuous route to a simple solution. The ability to allow people to reach their own conclusions in their own time is essential. Sometimes institutional time limitations will place constraints on the time for discussion and reflection. It is crucial to discuss these time limitations and devise a strategy for dealing with them.

Occasionally, the content produced by the group may conflict with the values and principles of the Social Action worker or of the school. These potential conflicts must be openly discussed and documented as far as is possible at the beginning of the process or as they arise. If the Social Action worker makes it clear that her or his personal principles and her or his reason for wanting to carry out this work involve a commitment to fairness, equality, and social justice, then that legitimizes any refusal to become embroiled in an activity that undermines those principles.

SOCIAL ACTION AND TEACHING

Sometimes Social Action workers face organizational pressure to adhere to more traditional methods. It is crucial for a Social Action worker to believe in the process and in the ability of people to effect change.

As the NWP teachers used Social Action and met to discuss their successes and less glorious moments, their confidence grew and their learning increased. At one of the later institutes, the participants created the following list of lessons learned, which shows how some previous concerns have been resolved through practice.

What We Know About Social Action That We Didn't Know Before

- Social Action is a dynamic process.

- Social Action is not predictable.

- It can take time.

- It can be messy.

- You have to accept that you do not know what the outcomes will be.

- Uncertainty is an important ingredient of the process.

- It can be difficult to create opportunities for Social Action unless you have some level of power in the institution in which you work.

- The process needs a balance between information and discovery.

- It is a fine line between facilitator and teacher.

- A teacher is *never* neutral.

- People in the same room can do the same [Social Action] training and yet can go away with completely different ideas of how to use it.

- The Social Action process builds communication skills.
- Social Action can fit with the curriculum.
- Conflict can be positive and is often part of the Social Action process.
- Divest from the product; concentrate on the process.
- You really have to believe in the principles, or it is an empty process.
- Social Action can be used in all sorts of different places.
- Group-building work is essential to the process.
- It takes time to understand Social Action in its entirety.

For some people, the tensions between Social Action and more traditional teaching remained a constant. Others felt validated by Social Action because the principles closely reflected their beliefs in student-centered learning. One teacher wrote, "It has been liberating for me to move from my traditional role of imparting knowledge to students to a revised role of creating knowledge alongside my students. This is not entirely new to me, but learning about Social Action has given me a structure for working in this way."

As teachers developed and adapted their Social Action practice to different situations, they learned from their own and others' experiences. For them, the Social Action approach *and* the challenges that they faced in using it with their students, colleagues, and communities engaged the power of their creativity.

Recommendations for the Classroom
Before You Start

JENNIE FLEMING, IAN BOULTON

If you are at all intrigued by the teacher accounts in this book and are wondering how to introduce Social Action into your work, this chapter is a good place to start. Social Action provides a logical framework designed by a teacher-facilitator that takes participants through the process in a safe and creative atmosphere. Like the rest of this volume, this chapter concentrates on teachers working with students, parents, and community members, but it bears remembering once again that Social Action can be done in a range of settings.

Following is a detailed explanation of the key concepts in Social Action: *facilitation, content,* and *process.* In addition, some guidelines on building community, setting up an appropriate environment, ensuring needed organizational support, and assessing the success of a Social Action project are included.

SOCIAL ACTION FACILITATION

A Social Action worker believes that young people have the skills and experience to change things that affect their lives; his or her job is to help young people decide what issues they wish to address. A teacher-facilitator must provide a safe environment in which to explore issues important to the young people as well as pose the right questions in the manner that will elicit the most honest answers. Effective facilitation relies on particular qualities and a consistency of approach rather than specific skills, training, or experience. Consider the following questions:

Are you able to ask questions rather than provide answers? Teacher-facilitators on youth-led projects reject the notion that young people have to be advised by adults or that adult wisdom is an essential ingredient of a Social Action project. This is replaced with the idea that young people need to be taken seriously and can provide their own solutions to their problems when given the opportunity. Effective facilitators, like good teachers, ask open-ended, searching questions.

Are you able to listen more than you talk? Teachers are used to being paid for what they know, for their input into group learning and discussions. Teacher-facilitators need to allow the young group members to fill in the silences.

Are you patient? Process-led work often means allowing groups to take what may seem like a circuitous route to a simple solution. The ability to bite your tongue, to not intervene, and to allow people to reach their own conclusions in their own time is essential. Sometimes teacher-facilitators face institutional time limitations that restrict their work. It is important that these limitations be discussed and that the young people agree among themselves on the appropriate time scales for their activities.

Do you believe it will work? Facilitation can be challenging. It is important that you believe in the process and the ability of young people to effect change and that you be able to defend the integrity of a youth-led process. This may be especially challenging for teachers when they are surrounded by other educators who are fiercely committed to more traditional methods or when organizational pressure dictates a particular outcome of the process. To be consistent in what you say to the group, your intentions must be clear from the beginning and remain so to the end of the project.

CONTENT IN SOCIAL ACTION

Young people know what is going on in their lives. Adults often make assumptions or guesses about young people's lives. In Social Action, we facilitate the process of young people or other group members discussing what is important to them. How we ask questions of young people is a crucial aspect of this; Social Action workers need to discipline themselves to ask questions that will develop a changing relationship between themselves and young people. Very often, adults ask young people questions that close conversations down or that assert authority over them. When we ask young people what adults ask them, they tell us that adults often start a "conversation" with them with questions like "What are you doing here?" "Do you know what will happen if you do that?" "Shouldn't you be in class?"—not inquiries they are going to respond to in a way that will go on to form discussion and dialogue. All discussions with young people should be viewed as having potential for change, so they should be purposeful and in keeping with the principles and process of Social Action. Asking Social Action questions is a means to starting useful conversations; it ensures that teacher-facilitators stay on the Social Action worker's side of the line (the left side of the Social Action process shown in Figure 13.3).

What is a Social Action question?

- A Social Action question is one to which you do not know the answer; the young person does.
- A Social Action question is one that you genuinely want answered.
- A Social Action question paves the way for an open discussion.

For example, a Social Action question in response to hearing that young people are joyriding might be something like this: What does it feel like? Isn't it scary? The question should solicit an answer that only the young person being asked will know, should not reveal a prejudgment on the part of the asker, and should help the facilitator get an idea of the motive for joyriding. Then the teacher-facilitator can consider with the young person other activities that address this motive; for example, are there other ways for young people to scare themselves or to enjoy the sensation of speed? This activity is *not* about letting young people off the hook for their behavior. It *is* about gaining a deeper understanding of young people and looking for workable solutions to community problems.

So by "content," we mean young people sharing their thoughts, ideas, beliefs, experiences, and opinions. Devising strategies and plans for action also make up the content of a youth-led project. Young people know what is going on in their lives, and they have the right to take action on their own behalf. Of course, sometimes content can be dictated by a specific subject. In a service-learning class, for instance, the group may only exist to engage in service learning. But in using Social Action, the group will be afforded the opportunity to do this entirely from their own perspectives and experiences.

Occasionally, the content produced by the group may conflict with the personal values and beliefs of the teacher-facilitator or the values and principles of the school. It is vital that potential conflicts be openly discussed and documented, to the extent possible, at the beginning of the process. If unforeseen conflicts arise, however, they must be addressed and discussed as soon as they occur. If the teacher-facilitator makes it clear from the beginning that her or his personal principles and reasons for wanting to do Social Action involve a commitment to fairness, equality, and social justice, this legitimizes a refusal to become embroiled in any activity that acts against these principles. Similarly, at the appropriate moment in the process, the teacher-facilitator should present the principles that govern the school and facilitate an exploration of possible tensions between those principles and the proposed actions of the group. Occasionally, it may be necessary for a teacher-facilitator to assist the group in negotiating with school officials.

THE SOCIAL ACTION PROCESS

In order for teacher-facilitators to help young people achieve their aims, they require a discipline, a logical way of working with the group. Youth-led activity is most effective when it goes through a series of key stages, maximizing opportunities to fully develop each stage in the ongoing process. It is the project staff's job to understand these stages and keep the group on track. The process should be well understood by the young people and should be explained to them at the outset. Concentrating on the process means that you can begin with a blank sheet of paper but still be clear about where the process will lead you.

BUILDING COMMUNITY IN SOCIAL ACTION WORK

Because group work lies at the heart of the Social Action approach, work during initial stages of a training session or project focuses on building a group identity. The facilitator works to create a sense of community in the group before taking participants through the process. Having a sense of trust and community allows the group members to support and challenge each other after the training is over and is one way that Social Action work enhances the sustainability of programs and organizations. A group's beginning stages establish its working culture. The beginning stages involve *identity, method,* and *purpose.*

Identity addresses the questions "Who are we?" and "What do our backgrounds have in common in terms of culture, job, ambition, age, gender, or other factors?" We have many tried and tested activities that we use to establish common ground in groups in a variety of situations. For example, a teacher-facilitator might ask people to tell the story behind their name. An even more interactive and dynamic exercise directs people to group themselves with others in various ways. For example, subgroups might be formed of people whose birthday is in the same month (a fact), those who share a taste for a particular kind of music (an opinion), or participants who have faith in the capacity of people to create change on their own (a belief). Obviously, while they are in such groups, the participants would talk with each other and establish what they have in common. (See, for example, the activities called "Metro Map" and "Naming the Group" in Part Three.)

Method involves figuring out how to work together as a group. How things are done is very important in Social Action work. Group members must create their own guidelines for how they will work together. Group maintenance is not just the job of the teacher-facilitators but is shared with all group members. Actively involving participants in deciding how they wish to work together begins to create responsibility for group maintenance.

Social Action workers often introduce the method stage by pointing out that once the group members have information about who is in the group, the next step is to determine how to work together as a group. Sometimes Social Action workers ask people to meet in small groups to consider what their hopes and fears are for the class or activity. Once people have communicated their hopes and fears to the rest of their group, each group's hopes and fears are passed on to another group. This second group thinks of actions that group members can take to ensure that the hopes are realized and the fears are not. These actions are then discussed in the big group, written up on flipchart paper, and left on the wall for the life of the group. (For an example of an exercise that helps a group determine its method of working together, see the Community Vocabulary activity in Part Three.)

The final stage of group building addresses *purpose*, asking questions such as the following: "What are we trying to achieve?" "When we meet, what do we try to do?" "What are our goals?" "What is our vision?" While all classes and some groups have broad aims and objectives that have been negotiated or set by outside agencies (curriculum goals, for example), each group must agree on their own specific goals and vision.

Many teacher-facilitators enable a group to agree on a purpose by creating a vision for the group (for example, see the activity called "Devising the Vision" in Part Three). Later, the vision can form the basis of the group's self-evaluation at the end of the session or class, when the group considers how much of what they set out to do has been achieved.

It is only after working with a group on identity, method, and purpose that Social Action workers move on to consider the Social Action process and the issues and concerns of the group. Only after those early stages have been completed do they know what the group members feel passionate about, what they disagree about, and what their aspirations are for the event, class, or workshop. Once facilitators have begun to gain this knowledge, they can begin to tailor the group work to the specific needs of the group.

How a group is set up or how a community is established has considerable influence on how members will deal with issues and problems that arise later in the process. Social Action workers attempt to create an environment in which people are listened to, asked to contribute their ideas, and encouraged to act on their suggestions in order to enable reflective groups and develop reflective practice.

THE SETTING FOR SOCIAL ACTION

Historically, Social Action workers in the United Kingdom had been reluctant to use schools as a setting for their projects with young people. This is because Social Action, in its early stages, was influenced by radical education writers such as Freire (1993), Holt (1970, 1976), and Illich (1973), who strongly challenged the notion that schools are places of learning. The work of the teachers from the National Writing Project has demonstrated that it is indeed possible to carry out Social Action projects in the classroom or school building. Still, it is worth considering what kind of impact the setting has on the work.

Spaces associated exclusively with formal learning or exclusively with social and recreational activity can be problematic for youth-led initiatives designed to create change. These spaces can also be problematic for parents or community members if they have had negative experiences with schooling or if they have experienced marginalization by the professionals working in schools. Ideally, a dedicated empty space with no connotations for the group that is available at all times should be used for Social Action projects. This is rarely possible, however. It is usually possible, though, to adapt an available space for group meetings or for the lifetime of the project. It is vital to ask yourself the following questions about your setting:

What other associations does the space have for the young people or community members? To help a Social Action project to be successful, its setting should be a place of work that is "owned" for the duration of the project by the young people themselves. If it feels like a place where you sit down and listen to adults, then the project will not work. On the other hand, if it feels like a private place for young people where adults are not to be allowed, then the project will not work, either. If the setting is designed for messing around, the project will not work. The setting for a Social Action project needs to be a place into which the young people can invite adults to work. This may be a space that the young people have decorated themselves or an adaptable space that can be made their own simply by rearranging furniture and putting group materials on the walls. It might also be a place associated with decision making in the school or the community; sometimes this kind of formal setting can show that the group is being taken seriously.

Is the space appropriate for the project to be undertaken? The teacher-facilitator should encourage the young people to critically examine the workspace, to decide whether it is suitable for their specific project and to consider its adaptability. Questions should include these: "Can we use our equipment in there?" "Can we make a mess?" "Can we use it when we wish?" "Can we leave our work on the walls?" "What happens if the group gets bigger?"

Will the times when you meet be dictated by the school or by the needs of the group? The first item on the Social Action agenda must be that the young people have some control over the logistics of meeting. They will understand that negotiation on such matters may be necessary, but they must not be left out of such discussions and presented with a decision that the facilitator has made on their behalf.

SOCIAL ACTION WITHIN INSTITUTIONS AND ORGANIZATIONS

As in all effective community or educational work, accountability is a key principle of youth-led work. Teacher-facilitators need to be able to set goals and expect outcomes, to decide what can be measured and how they are going to measure it. At a program level, we can clearly measure, for example, attendance. But here we must measure it against young people's attendance patterns in other types of groups. Is it an improvement on the group members' attendance record for other school activities or in other formal educational settings? Similarly, with regard to attainment, an important question might be how the achievements of the individuals and the group compare with what they have achieved elsewhere. The organization must decide on these ways of measurement, set clear boundaries, and then trust in the process. *For a Social Action school project to be successful, principals, administrators, and other staff members must avoid actions that get in the way of effective participation.* Their conduct must

- Help teacher-facilitators to see the work through, to finish what has been started

- Not isolate teacher-facilitators

- Ensure that the culture of the school can comfortably contain this initiative and that other people attached to the institution understand what is going on and can see it as part of a whole

A SUCCESSFUL SOCIAL ACTION PROJECT IS . . .

So what does it mean to say that Social Action is happening? How will a teacher-facilitator know that Social Action is "working" with the students? A successful Social Action project is a collaborative partnership that changes the role of the teacher from expert and leader to partner and teacher-facilitator. It encourages self-directed group work, building on the strengths of the group, allowing participants to set their own agenda, and respecting local knowledge. While success in Social Action terms measures collective achievement, there are also individual gains. When asked what they gained from being involved in Social Action projects, student participants cited ownership, pride, increased self-esteem, sharpened communication skills, and the confidence to question the dominance of positions of authority.

Because Social Action is process-oriented, its success, like the success of teaching, can be judged in many different ways. While group success in achieving the chosen goal is one obvious measure of success, participants can gain a tremendous amount from the process, whether they reach their goal or fall short. Here are some equally important ways to gauge the success of a Social Action project (Mullender and Ward, 1991):

During the project

- The group takes collective action to address an issue they have identified.

- Over time, group members assume increasing responsibility for making decisions and executing tasks while the teacher-facilitator moves further into the background. Ultimately, group members continue to work after the prescribed period of facilitation. (This can be difficult to achieve in classes and other temporary settings, but it's an ideal to keep in mind.)

After the project

- Group members continue to use their shared strength and conviction, now acknowledging their right and their capacity to change their lives.

- Group members make connections with people beyond their immediate group, recognizing the importance of these links to taking further action.

- Social Action workers transfer the wider relevance of the Social Action process and principles to different settings.

The following section contains activities that are the building blocks of a Social Action session or project.

Good luck!

PART THREE

Stuff You Can Try

Activities for Social Action

For those of you interested in introducing Social Action to the young people with whom you work, this section provides suggested exercises you can use with the Social Action process.

As we hope this volume has demonstrated, Social Action is not simply a collection of techniques and activities; it is a clear process of addressing problems and issues as a community. Within that process, Social Action principles guide all that the teacher-facilitator does. However, there are certain exercises and activities that Social Action workers have found particularly useful over time, and many of these were shared during the cross-national events that were part of the NWP-CSA collaboration. In addition, as they developed their roles as teacher-facilitators, the project participants developed new exercises and adapted exercises they had already used in their classrooms to fit the principles and process of Social Action. This section provides a window into the concrete activities that they used as they worked with young people.

The suggested activities, of course, are just that—suggestions. You should not feel restricted to using these activities, nor should you feel you must use them exactly as they are. A key to facilitating Social Action work is to get to know your group and understand what they want to achieve; then you can adopt, adapt, develop, or create exercises that will help them meet their goals. The central principle behind these activities is that Social Action workers are not leaders but facilitators. In Social Action activities the content comes from the group. As a teacher-facilitator, you are trying to create a process that enables a group to identify the issues and concerns that they face, understand why these exist, explore how they can take action to change things, take that action, and reflect on what has happened, all in a cyclical process. All the activities in this section are designed to enable the young people you work with to provide the content of Social Action, to facilitate their discussion of the things that are important in their lives, to help them analyze why things are as they are, and to help them consider how they can take action to change things.

Finally, remember that Social Action is a process with an interlocking set of principles, so it is crucial that all activities be in keeping with the principles of Social Action. Promoting social justice and challenging inequality and oppression are central to Social Action. Social Action is derived from a recognition that all young people have skills, experience, and understanding and are experts in their own lives; that all people have rights, including the right to be heard, the right to define the issues facing them, and the right to take action on their own behalf; that injustice and oppression are complex issues rooted in social policy, the environment, and the economy; and that people working collectively can be powerful and their collective action should be encouraged. If we keep these principles in mind, many group activities can be seen as useful and as advancing Social Action.

What follows is a typical Social Action sequence of activities, designed to create a community that can identify, analyze, and take action to address the problems it faces or other matters that are important to the group. This process could happen over a three-day event or a summer school, or it could form the basis of a term's project with young people on a community activity or in the classroom. An activity can take a couple of hours or many weeks to complete. Yet the activities should not be used in an ad hoc manner; they should be part of a purposeful plan that is linked to the what, why, how, action, and reflection stages of the Social Action process and designed for the specific group of people you are working with, so that each activity builds on and takes further the content created by the young people in the previous activity and discussions. Finally, while these are activities that the teacher-facilitators in this collaboration found useful in the classroom, they can also be used in community settings and with adults as well as young people. They are flexible and adaptable activities, and because they are designed to enable the participants to provide the content, they can be used in a wide range of settings with a wide variety of people.

Each activity is described in the following pages. We have not been prescriptive about how or at what exact stage in the process they should be used because many of the exercises can be adapted and used at different stages. However, in the following list, we have grouped the activities into sections (Activities for Creating Community, Activities for Defining and Analyzing Problems, Activities for Planning Action, and Activities for Reflection) and indicated the stage of community building or the stage of the Social Action process at which they might be particularly useful and appropriate to use. But do not feel bound by these suggestions. Experiment!

Activities for Creating Community

These activities allow group members to get to know each other and develop a common identity.

Activity	Stage
Metro Map	Identity
Naming the Group	Identity
Community Vocabulary	Method
Devising the Vision	Purpose
How We Behave in Groups	Method

Activities for Defining and Analyzing Problems

The Social Action facilitator uses these activities to encourage group members to express what is happening in their lives: What are their issues, problems, and concerns? What makes them angry, frightened, frustrated, and happy? Some of these activities allow community members to engage in analysis and to present their understanding of the problems facing them. It also helps them to discover the most effective point of intervention, the place at which it is possible to make changes that will affect the final outcomes.

Activity	Stage
Movie Poster	What
Four Faces	Why*
But Why?	Why
Codes	Why
Changing Your Mind	Why or How
Sculpts	Why or How

*This activity could be used at various stages, depending on the statements used.

Activities for Planning Action

The group members decide on an action that they want to take to address the issues they have identified.

Activity	Stage
The Three C's	How
SWOT	How
Ideal Specimen	How
Force Field Analysis	How or Action
Worst Nightmare	How or Action
Now/Soon/Later	Action

Activities for Reflection

These activities provide opportunities for critical reflection that enables students to learn from their experiences and to plan future actions for change.

Activity	Stage
The Swimming Pool	Reflection
Messages	How or Reflection

At the end of a group session, series of sessions, or project it is a good idea to return to the vision and community vocabulary that were created at the start. This allows the group to see how well they have worked toward their vision and what they have achieved, as well as whether they have worked together in the way suggested in the community vocabulary.

Activity Metro Map

Purpose

- To understand others' backgrounds
- To answer these questions:
  - What brought us together?
  - What do we have in common?

How We Do It

1. Divide participants into small groups of four to eight people. Give each group a piece of flipchart paper and a different color marker for each member. Show what the small group should do by drawing a circle in the center of a piece of paper and write in the circle the only thing that you know to be true about the group members: that they have all, for some reason, turned up in this room. Their final destination on the metro is this training session, class, conference, or meeting. What brought them here? Which significant events in their own personal history led them ultimately to this place? Ask each individual in the room to identify three crucial events in her own life that led her here and to draw a line from the edge of the flipchart to the final destination, marking the three events as stops on a map.

2. Ask the small groups to allow each member to take a turn and explain to the small group what she is writing and thinking as she marks her stops.

3. When the map is complete, ask the group to consider two questions:

   - What do your backgrounds have in common? Are there any factors you can identify that led several of you down this path?
   - What is different about your routes? How divergent are the paths that led to this room?

Variations, Adaptations, and Developments

It is possible to use this exercise in one big group if the facilitator wants to use it for team building or thinks that full disclosure is important to the group's process.

Why We Like It

This activity acknowledges commonality and difference between participants, while acknowledging that their final destination has ultimately been the same. It allows participants to identify themselves more accurately as individuals rather than just "teachers" or "street kids."

When You Can Use It

This activity works well at the very beginning of a large-scale event. It can also be used during a training session, event, or semester when the group needs to be reminded of where they came from and that they have a common purpose, or when commonality or diversity is important to the group's process and is in danger of being forgotten.

Issues to Consider

The facilitator must acknowledge that some events that led participants to the room may be of a personal nature and so they may not want to share them. Advise group members that in this case, they should write that "something happened" without describing it.

Materials

Flipchart, pens of many different colors.

Source

Devised by Cathy Burdge for a training session called "Working with Street Children" as part of the Centre for Social Action's work on deinstitutionalization of children's services in Ukraine.

Activity Naming the Group

Purpose

- To explore identity
- To create common identity
- To bring people together

How We Do It

1. Divide the large group into smaller groups of four to six people. Participants take turns at telling the other members of their small group two things:

   - Something they are proud of
   - Something it is important for other people to know about them

2. When everybody has had a turn, ask the small groups to think about the things that have been said and identify something the individuals in their small group have in common. They should use this as the basis of their decision for a group name. What do they wish to call themselves?

Variations, Adaptations, and Developments

Sometimes it is helpful to ask the small groups to imagine that they are in a band and are giving it a name.

Why We Like It

This activity allows group members to choose an identity for themselves that is not necessarily how they are typically described or identified. It can be surprising and fun.

When You Can Use It

This activity can be used at the beginning of an event or group project.

Issues to Consider

When choosing their name, the group should consider that their name may become public during the course of a longer project. But keep in mind that the group may later decide to no longer be identified by the name they choose.

Materials

Flipchart paper and markers, for posting the group names.

Source

Devised by Ian Boulton and Jennie Fleming for a session of the Centre for Social Action Summer School.

Activity Community Vocabulary

Purpose

- To decide how participants will talk with each other
- To set language boundaries
- To look at good and bad experiences in groups

How We Do It

1. Divide the large group into small groups containing at least three but no more than seven members. Ask each group to think about the session, workshop, or class in which they are participating and their opinions, expectations, hopes, and fears about what is going to take place.

2. Ask the small groups to produce two lists of words or short phrases titled "Words We Want to Hear" and "Words We Don't Want to Hear."

3. As the groups are making their lists, prepare two pieces of flipchart paper with headings under which you will transcribe the lists. Call on each group to share three words or phrases at a time until all of the contributions are listed under their respective categories.

4. Post the papers on the wall of the room and explain to the group that the "Words We Want to Hear" illustrate the way the large group wants to conduct discussions and communicates how group members want to be treated. These desired words also show how the group wants to be viewed.

5. The other list tells everyone what the group wants to avoid: which words they find offensive, boring, confusing, or off-putting. Explain that this second list often reveals something about previous negative experiences that group members have encountered in similar settings.

6. Finally, mention that the lists can be expanded throughout the process as discussions develop and more words attract or repel group members.

Why We Like It

A community vocabulary helps set language boundaries in workshops or classes. It gives group members ownership of the language that will be used in a direct fashion. It also gives the facilitator clues about the group's preferred methods of working, past experiences, and ambitions for the process ahead. Finally, it is organic and develops throughout the session.

When You Can Use It

This activity can be used in any learning setting, preferably at the beginning of a process.

Issues to Consider

The second list is not meant to be a form of censorship, but merely an indicator of the group's intentions regarding the verbal content of the course. It should be taken seriously, but treated lightly if one of the words is used by a group member.

Materials

Flipchart and markers.

Activity Devising the Vision

Purpose

- To decide on definitive purposes for the group
- To negotiate and agree on a common purpose
- To set a standard for success

How We Do It

1. At the beginning of a class, semester, or session, invite each participant to write down the three things that they wish to achieve by its end.

2. Each participant shares this list with a partner, and the pair then negotiates a joint list of three goals they wish to achieve based on similarity, preferred wording, and importance.

3. Each pair then joins up with another pair, and another round of negotiation takes place, producing a refined list of three things between the four participants. These are then fed back to the whole group.

4. Take note of everything that is said and then begin a whole-group negotiation on the three things the group will achieve by the end of the project or term. The final three are written on a flipchart and placed prominently on the wall.

5. Explain that the group will revisit this list at the end of the course and decide to what extent it has achieved its aims.

Why We Like It

This exercise introduces the notion that negotiation is an integral element of group work. It sets a clear, agreed-on, and realistic agenda that will aid the facilitator in planning and the group in maintaining focus. It helps to legitimize some discussion and activity and to outlaw others. It results in an aid to evaluation devised by group members themselves.

When You Can Use It

This activity can be used at the beginning of a class or workshop.

Issues to Consider

The most difficult part of the exercise is the final negotiation. This needs to move along briskly, without ignoring participants' ideas or imposing the facilitator's. Sometimes it may be necessary to add a fourth aim, to save time. The facilitator may need to remind the group several times that this exercise creates a vision for the course, not for the primary content of the course. The exercise is meant to encourage ambition but not set unrealistic expectations.

Materials

Flipchart and markers.

Activity: How We Behave in Groups

Purpose

- To explore individual behavior
- To examine the positive and negative aspects of different ways of behaving in groups

How We Do It

1. Using all available wall space, attach six pieces of paper to the walls, spaced as far apart as possible. On each piece of paper, two words are written:

   Intellectual/Thinking

   Emotional/Feeling

   Light-hearted/Joking

   Argumentative/Challenging

   Quiet/Listening

   Practical/Doing

2. Ask participants to think about their own behavior as individuals when they are in the company of other people in an organized setting. Instruct participants to consider which of the words on the walls describe their typical behavior as a group participant. With what words does each individual *most* identify? Ask group members to stand under the paper that best reflects their behavior in groups.

3. Once the participants have assembled in smaller groups under each piece of flipchart paper, ask them to consider the following two questions and discuss them with the people they are standing with.

   - What is helpful about this behavior in groups?
   - What is unhelpful about this behavior in groups?

   Give the groups ten minutes for this discussion.

4. Ask each group in turn to share what they learned or talked about with the entire group.

Variations, Adaptations, and Developments

During the feedback, the facilitator may ask the group, "Who do you think has the most difficulty with this way of behaving? Where is the potential for conflict in the group?"

Why We Like It

This activity allows participants to reflect on their own behavior and to acknowledge how they contribute to group work. It pushes them to consider the ways in which they may sometimes be difficult to work with. It also can help the facilitator to know the participants and inform how he or she works with the group to ensure the participation of all group members.

When You Can Use It

After doing the Community Vocabulary and Devising the Vision activities, this process can help the group identify how to work together in more detail. It can also be used at any stage during the process when the facilitator (or a group member) realizes that the group is not functioning at its full capacity.

Issues to Consider

- It is important to stress that the mode of behavior chosen by the members in this activity is not a label that they will be stuck with throughout the rest of the workshop, class, or project. They are being asked to identify with one way of behaving just for this activity.
- Group members must be self-critical as well as explore what is helpful about the various behaviors. If this is not happening, the facilitator needs to change the focus to what is unhelpful about any given behavior—for example, "Yes, jokers can be fun in a group, but let's think about what people may find difficult about people who frequently participate by making jokes."

Materials

Flipcharts, markers, masking tape, a large room.

Activity Movie Poster

Purpose

- To decide issues
- To create an agenda
- To explore how the group sees things
- To express what is important in participants' lives

How We Do It

1. Ask people to divide into two or more groups, depending on the size of the whole group. Ask group members to imagine that a movie will be made of what happens in their lives in their neighborhood, community, school, family, or other groups or settings that are important to them. Participants should consider what is going on in their lives, including the positive and negative things that happen where they live. What makes them angry or happy? What are they afraid of? What frustrates them? Ask them to think about what would be in the movie about their lives.

2. Ask each group to create a poster to advertise their movie, representing the things they have been discussing. Each group will draw a poster on which the only written words should be the title. You might suggest that participants consider what they want people to understand about their lives by looking at their poster.

3. Once all of the groups have completed their drawings, display them. Take each poster in turn, and ask the groups that did not create the poster what they see while the creators listen quietly. Ask a variety of questions that get other groups to describe the other posters: What do they see in it? What does the title mean to them? Do they see themselves in the poster? Make a list of the responses on chart paper. After you have made a thorough list, ask the group who made the poster whether what people have seen is what they intended, and whether they think anything has been left out. Everything that is said is valid and is recorded, even if it is not what the artists intended.

4. Once the first poster has been fully discussed, move on to the next one until all posters have been considered.

5. After all of the posters have been discussed, the list is put on the wall. This is a list of problems and concerns that will form the group's agenda.

Variations, Adaptations, and Developments

This exercise can also be used with professionals. You might ask them to consider the lives of the people they work with. It is important to develop the exercise by using the information gained.

Why We Like It

- People are not used to expressing themselves through drawing, and the exercise may help participants to articulate different aspects of their lives than they would if they answered verbally.
- This activity creates camaraderie.
- It is particularly freeing for adults.
- It is fun.
- There is no need for reading or writing at this stage of the exercise.
- The pictures can stay in the room.
- This activity is good in bilingual settings.

When You Can Use It

This is a versatile exercise that is appropriate for use with many groups. We have used it with such varied groups as street children in Moscow, teachers in America, and young people on estates in Britain. (Estates are called *housing projects* in the United States.)

Issues to Consider

- The exercise can take some time because people need to discuss, agree, and decide how to depict things and then actually draw them, and then additional time is needed to discuss the posters.
- It is important to reassure people that this is not an artistic competition and that any quality of drawing is fine.
- This is a good exercise to use near the beginning of a group or course because it lets participants tell you about what is important in their lives.

- It is crucial that information about people's lives be used; this is not an activity for the sake of it.

Materials

Pens of many colors, flipchart paper, masking tape for putting posters on the wall.

Source

Centre for Social Action and the Guinness Trust, 2000.

Activity Four Faces

Purpose

- To uncover opinions
- To recognize a variety of opinions
- To allow participants to explore their opinions and to change their minds

How We Do It

1. Create controversial statements for your group. It is best to do this once you know the group and have been listening to them and hearing their differences of opinion and unresolved issues. The statements need to be carefully worded to allow for difference of interpretation and opinion. If you don't know the group, use statements that have worked well with similar groups. You want to provoke debate and discussion, not deliberately foster conflict. Always have more statements on hand than you need and have some idea about which ones you will use, but make the final decision about which ones to use as you listen to the discussion.

   Here are some examples of statements we have used in the past with groups of teachers or students:

   - You learn more in school than in the rest of your life.
   - Education should always be enjoyable.
   - It is important for learning that a teacher be liked by his or her students.
   - It is essential for learning that a teacher like his or her students.
   - It is detrimental to learning if a student does not like his or her teachers.
   - It is possible to do Social Action in a classroom.
   - Your personal beliefs as a teacher get in the way of the learning of the people you are working with.
   - Adults learn as much from working with young people as young people learn from adults.
   - Education should prepare young people for employment.
   - Literacy means different things to teachers than students.

- Teachers have a responsibility to students beyond the classroom.

- We can't do anything about colleagues who are not interested in empowerment.

2. Draw four faces with very different expressions on four pieces of paper: one very happy, one happy, one slightly unhappy, and one very unhappy face. Explain the faces and what they mean.

3. Read a statement. Ask people to stand by the face that best reflects their opinion or level of agreement with the statement. People must express their personal viewpoint. For example, if someone personally agrees strongly with the statement, they would stand by very smiley face.

4. Ask people at each face to talk among themselves about why they have chosen where to stand and what they want say to the others to encourage agreement. The group's viewpoint can be presented in a variety of ways:

- Ask someone who hasn't spoken before to make a statement for the group.

- Ask the group members to discuss it among themselves and choose one person to present their views.

- Ask a group to select three main points they want to make.

5. After the discussion is over, ask the groups to discuss among themselves all the points of view heard and see if they want to review their position. People are encouraged to talk and share and change their mind, given others' points of view. Remember to let people move about if they want to change their view. It is not uncommon for people to take a number of positions before finally deciding what their position on a given statement is.

It is possible to vary the tone of this exercise considerably. You can suggest that group members actively persuade others to join them or ask them to just state their opinion and see if that encourages people to move.

The exercise can take a very long time, allowing for a lot of discussion and debate, or it can be a quick opinion finder.

6. It is good to end with a consensus statement (if you can find one), because participants can become heated and even upset during the process.

Variations, Adaptations, and Developments

You can connect this discussion to the action stage. For example, following the activity, ask "OK, so what does this mean we need to do?" or "What tips would you have for this situation?"

Why We Like It

This activity can help a group explore relevant issues and opinions. People express an opinion by placing themselves near a face or expression, so all people can participate without having to speak.

When You Can Use It

This exercise can be used with virtually any group, including young children or adults. It is extremely versatile and can help facilitate a quick, fun discussion or a lengthy, serious debate.

Issues to Consider

- It is important that the facilitator consider the wording of the statements carefully.
- Sometimes people will feel isolated.
- This activity can get heated, but that can be a good thing.
- Not often, but occasionally, the whole group agrees with each other. This may be genuine consensus, but you may wish to warn group members to be wary of the impulse to follow the crowd.
- Rehearse well how you will explain what the four faces represent; it can be confusing to the participants.
- This activity is not about creating conflict but about airing opinions.

Materials

The statements, paper for the four faces, masking tape, and a space for people to move around in.

Activity But Why?

Purpose

- To analyze issues
- To look at causes of issues, concerns, or problems
- To consider the consequences of not taking action

How We Do It

This activity is a two-stage process that allows a group to consider the consequences and causes of a situation. Stage 1 explores the consequences of problems: what may happen if the group doesn't act. Stage 2 is a discussion of why the problem exists.

Stage 1

1. Have the group agree on a key problem or issue for which they want to investigate ramifications and attendant problems. In this first stage, the group explores the scale of the problem and paints a picture of just how destructive the problem would be if no action were taken to address it. (After all, if not much would happen if you didn't tackle it, then you might want to tackle something else.)

2. Write the problem that the group has agreed on in the center of a piece of flipchart paper. Ask one group member to volunteer to take the interrogating role throughout the exercise; after each answer to the question, he or she writes the answer on the paper, reads it out loud, and asks the question, "But why?" So to start, the interrogator reads the problem out loud, followed by the question, "But why?" For example, the interrogator might ask, "Bad relationships between young people and the police are a problem, but why?" A possible response is "Young people get blamed." The interrogator then would say, "Young people getting blamed is a problem, but why?" and write the next response down, producing a connected line. This line of inquiry is explored until it either peters out or reaches a logical conclusion (for example, "The young people end up in prison"). Each line represents a string of related consequences and should go as far as people can suggest those consequences. (See page 129.)

3. A line is finished when the group can think of no more consequences. Once one line has been completed, the group starts a new line by stating the original problem and once again asking "But why?" Take the same example, "Bad relationships between young people and the police are a problem, but why?" This time the response is "They are not safe." In this way, as many lines are produced as possible. There should be at least four or five lines.

4. Ask the group members to consider what they have created on the flipchart. They should consider whether there are any connections between the consequences and, if so, draw connecting lines between them. Some words or concepts may recur on different lines; draw connecting lines between these, creating a web. The task is to look at commonalities between consequences; this will give clues about what is important and indicate which consequences are most likely if the problem is not addressed. Once again, it is the group's opinions that matter; there are no correct answers. At this stage, the group members are not trying to resolve the problem or look for a definite answer; they are exploring perceptions.

BUT WHY - FIRST STAGE

↗ prison → no job

commit crime
↑
no job
↑
won't be trusted
↑
get into trouble
↑
get blamed
↖

BAD RELATIONSHIPS
BETWEEN YOUNG PEOPLE
AND THE POLICE ARE
A PROBLEM.

↓   ↓
not safe   parents test
↓   police
scared   ↓
↓   won't believe us
behave badly | show off   ↓
↓   fall out
get into trouble   ↓
↓   leave house
bad reputation   ↓
↓   no money
won't be trusted   ↓
↓   no job
kicked out of house ──────────→   ↓
                                   crime
                         prison ↙   ↓

5. The next step is to identify a possible point of intervention. Ask the group members to consider the diagram they have created and think about where they can make a difference, what they feel comfortable working on, and what they can practically address.

6. Have the group pick one consequence to do further work on, then continue to stage 2.

Stage 2

In the second stage, the group will move from looking at consequences of the problem to examining causes, focusing on the consequence that has been chosen as the point of intervention.

1. Take a fresh piece of flipchart paper, write the chosen consequence at the top, and ask the group members to examine the causes of the consequence in a linear fashion: "This is a problem; what causes it?" Say, for example, that the consequence the group has chosen is "young people getting kicked out of the house." You might say, "Young people getting kicked out of the house—this is a problem. What causes it?" A suggestion from the group might be "Poor relationship with parents." You would then ask, "What causes bad relationships with parents?" A suggestion might be "They speak different languages, use different words." You would then ask, "What is the cause of this?" The response might be, "They live in different worlds," and so on.

2. There is usually more than one root cause for a problem. If the group members believe that the first causal analysis doesn't show the full complexity of the situation, they can run step 1 again on a fresh piece of flipchart paper in order to get a fuller picture and a more comprehensive analysis of the causes.

3. Have the group members look at the linear routes they've created on the chart paper. Which words suggest gaps or action? Pick out words about action (*understand, clarify, prioritize, perceptions, explain,* and so on). Ask the group members to find a starting point—any starting point—for actions they themselves can plan to carry out.

4. The group is now in a position to develop appropriate strategies and tactics to tackle the problem they've identified, based on the analysis they have

undertaken. Other activities can be used to develop these plans and ideas. In the preceding case, the group might, for example, choose to develop a plan to aid communication between young people and their parents.

Why We Like It

This activity explores the causes of problems. Without analysis, understanding can be shallow and group members might blame people rather than see the complexity of a situation. This activity encourages people to think about the causes of a problem or issue rather than moving straight from identification of a problem to trying to solve it.

When You Can Use It

This is an excellent activity to use once group members have identified the problem or issue they want to address and then need to consider *why* it exists (what causes it) so that they can target their actions most effectively.

Issues to Consider

- This can be a complicated activity, so all instructions need to be very clear. It is worth going through an example with the whole group; everyone needs to understand how the process works before going into small groups.
- It is helpful if a small group can gather around a piece of chart paper on the floor, on the wall, or on a large table.

Materials

Chart paper and pens.

Source

Adapted from Hope and Timmel, 1999.

Activity Codes

Purpose

- To acquire a deeper understanding of a group's views
- To structure an examination of the discussion about a topic
- To analyze a situation or the causes of a problem

How We Do It

1. Present an image for the group to consider in silence. The image may be a drawing, a photograph, or a mime. Inform group members that they will be taken through a series of questions after the presentation. They are not to discuss the image with each other until you begin to ask the questions.

2. Slowly and carefully, ask the following questions:

   - What is happening?
   - Does this happen in real life?
   - Why does it happen?
   - Where are you in this?
   - What needs to change?

   The pace of the discussion should be slow, with the facilitator leaving long pauses between questions to allow the group to further reflect on the image and the responses given by fellow members at each stage of questioning. Follow-up questions should be kept to a minimum and used only for clarity—for example, "Could you repeat that?"

Variations, Adaptations, and Developments

Anything can be a code. It is possible to use a song or a poem or role-play—for example, a short monologue, a skit, or a sculpt (see the "Sculpts" activity later in this section). We find, however, that the quiet brought about by consideration of a silent visual image aids the conversation that follows.

Why We Like It

This is a thoughtful exercise that allows considered discussion of an issue in an oblique or even abstract way. The image should provoke relevant thoughts and comments but remain open to any interpretation. This exercise helps to personalize issues for individual participants.

When You Can Use It

This activity can be used once an agenda has been established and the group members feel safe with each other. They are particularly useful as a lead-in to the "why" stage.

Issues to Consider

The image needs to be chosen carefully. It should be ambiguous. It should have some allusion to power relationships and decision making. If a photograph is used, it is impossible to obscure all reference to geography, race, gender, age, or class. Photographs can make group members pay attention to small details and provoke serious, intense discussion if chosen carefully. Participants are sometimes taken by surprise by the emotions evoked during this exercise. The facilitator needs to be prepared for this and should adopt a suitable tone and pace.

Materials

Images that are suitable for use as codes; they should be ambiguous and open to a variety of interpretations. Websites can sometimes provide interesting photos. (Be sure to check on copyright issues if you are reproducing material.)

Source

Adapted from Hope and Timmel, 1999.

Activity Changing Your Mind

Purpose

- To ask the following questions:
  - How do people learn?
  - What has helped us to learn in the past?
- To discover ways of learning through role play

How We Do It

1. Ask people to think, by themselves, of a time as a child or young person when they changed their mind about something that was important to them. It needs to be something they are prepared to share. It doesn't have to be too personal. The focus will be on the circumstances that led to the change—who was involved, how it happened. It is the process of changing their mind that is important, not what they changed their mind about.

2. Ask them to think about the following questions:

   - What was the topic, and what was your original position?
   - Under what circumstances did you change your mind?
   - Who or what was involved?
   - What was your relationship with them?
   - What was your new position?

3. Have participants form small groups. Mention that changing one's mind can be seen as a learning process and that they will be looking at their experience to discover what can be understood about learning. Have all participants share their examples and consider what lessons about how people learn can be drawn from their experiences. Then they need to agree on three lessons about how people learn and write them on a flipchart page.

4. The final stage of the exercise is to consider the implications of these lessons for facilitators and educators and imagine what actions they can take or build

into their practice to take those implications into account. Ask the participants to consider these questions:

- What do your discoveries and insights tell us as teachers or students?
- What do they tell us about how people learn?
- What do we need to do to take this understanding into account?

Variations, Adaptations, and Developments

It is possible for people to role-play an example, to show the processes and people that can be involved when people are learning and when they change their mind about important issues.

Why We Like It

This activity allows people to reflect on their own experience and draws out some general lessons about how people learn.

When You Can Use It

We often use this activity in train-the-trainer workshops or work with teachers, but it is equally applicable to work with students.

Issues to Consider

It can be helpful to offer an example (one that doesn't give all the answers) or ask for a volunteer.

Materials

Flipchart paper, markers.

Activity Sculpts

Purpose

- To consider problems without using words
- To find out what needs to change
- To get everyone involved in the process

How We Do It

1. Ask group members to think about one of the issues that have been uncovered during the "what" phase of their work. Divide participants into small groups, and ask them to present the problem in the form of a body sculpture—that is, a still and silent picture using only the people in the group and no props or words.

2. Each group presents its sculpture in turn. The other groups observe the picture and are asked what it portrays and how it could be changed so that the problem presented is solved. The facilitator then invites participants who are not in the sculpture to get up and physically move the people around in the sculpture so that the situation is improved. The new sculpture should illustrate the situation after effective action has been taken.

Variations, Adaptations, and Developments

In one variation, small groups are asked to show sculpts that depict three phases:

- The current situation
- The transitional period while action is taking place
- The situation in the future

In this variation, the group members themselves, rather than the observers, provide the solutions. This format is used to focus on the period before the chosen strategy is completed. This is best used after the "how" has been decided, so that the group can examine the difficulties they will face.

Why We Like It

This exercise is active and creative and places the burden for solving the problem on the onlookers, not on those who have identified it. The exercise also works as a form of consultation; it gives groups hope and acts as a spur to action. It is non-verbal, so it does not include discussion of the problem. The only discussion takes place after the second sculpture is completed and the group is asking, "How can we get from Picture A to Picture B?"

When You Can Use It

This is most useful at the beginning of the "how" phase.

Issues to Consider

- Sometimes participants in the sculptures try to hold impossible positions for a long time. The facilitator should allow them to rest while the onlookers are deciding on their actions.

- The exercise also involves close physical contact and being manipulated by other group members. People who feel uncomfortable with this aspect are allowed to opt out of the physical part of the activity and can still join in the discussion.

Materials

None.

Source

Everyman Youth Theatre, Liverpool, 1972.

Activity The Three C's

Purpose

- To identify who might be involved in or have an influence on a group's project
- To consider the following questions:
  - Who will help us?
  - Who will stand in our way?
- To begin to develop action plans

How We Do It

1. Once a group has agreed on a goal, ask them to think of three groups of people:

   - People who agree with their goal and who will help them
   - People whom they need to convince
   - People who will oppose them

   Ask the group to produce lists of these people under the following headings: Cooperate, Campaign, and Confront.

2. Ask the group to consider that more people may be on their side than is immediately obvious and to consider who besides themselves would benefit if the group's goal is achieved. Would there be benefits for their parents? For journalists looking for a story? Similarly, the group should consider that those who will try to stop them from achieving their goal may not be people who disagree with them; they may be people who envy the group or people who are competing for funds or attention.

3. Insist that the participants pay attention to the middle group when devising their action plan. Participants need to think about who they need to convince and how they are going to do it.

Variations, Adaptations, and Developments

This activity can be done alongside the SWOT analysis (see the next activity) by asking the group to leave people out of the SWOT and just focus on institutions, events, qualities, and so on. The group then uses the Three C's activity to concentrate on the people involved. Actions to increase strengths, lessen weaknesses, use opportunities, and diminish threats can then be placed on the diagram for the Force Field Analysis activity. Similarly, actions that will help to bring the unconvinced over to the group's side can be added.

Why We Like It

This activity is an accessible way to introduce political realities to the group at a key stage. There will always be opposition to change, and the opposition's motives will not always be easy to identify. There will always be activists and proponents of change who will be easy to attract. The task of convincing those who are undecided that the change you seek is worthwhile or in their interest is the key to creating a movement for change. This notion helps young people to solidify their thinking, to think tactically, and to plan negotiation.

When You Can Use It

You can use this exercise to help create the action plan during the "how" stage. It can be used alongside the Force Field Analysis activity and the SWOT activity.

Issues to Consider

The Three C's introduces outside personalities and influences into the group's consideration. The facilitator's job in this activity is to ask questions that lead the group to consider the outside world rather than posit her or his own opinions. It is vital that construction of the lists and the discussions about them be conducted in a disciplined, focused way. This is not an opportunity for group members to malign people who disagree with them.

Materials

Flipchart, markers.

Activity SWOT

Purpose

- To analyze and reflect on current or future activities
- To plan an event
- To evaluate a group's work

How We Do It

1. Begin by explaining what SWOT stands for:

   S: strengths

   W: weaknesses

   O: opportunities

   T: threats

   With the group, identify the plan or event that they will analyze.

2. Put four pieces of flipchart paper on the wall, one for each part of the SWOT analysis. Ask group members to consider each of the four aspects and write their ideas on the sheets. Alternatively, have people write their ideas on sticky notes and place them on the appropriate chart.

3. When everyone is finished, go through each sheet with the group as a whole, or divide the group into four and have participants work in small groups. Have the participants discuss ideas and reach consensus or rank ideas by level of importance.

Variations, Adaptations, and Developments

It is OK to change the words in order to help the group understand better. For example, you could state the areas this way:

Strengths: What was good?

Weaknesses: What was bad?

Opportunities: What could happen now?

Threats: What might stop things from happening?

Why We Like It

This activity can be used as a planning or a reflection exercise to help a group either evaluate the tasks it has been involved in or look forward to future work.

When You Can Use It

This activity can be used during the "how" or the "reflect" stage of the Social Action process.

Issues to Consider

Make sure all group members are able to participate and that their ideas are represented.

Materials

Flipchart paper, marker pens, sticky notes, masking tape.

Source

Dynamix, 2002.

Activity: Ideal Specimen

Purpose

- To explore skills and have fun
- To identify training needs
- To decide on roles

How We Do It

1. Divide participants into groups of four or five, and ask them to think about the qualities or skills required to fill the particular role or job they are considering—to dream up the ideal specimen.

2. Next, participants need to think of how they can represent these qualities and attributes visually. Each group draws its ideal version of, for example, a Social Action worker, a police officer, or a student or teacher, discussing and agreeing on what needs to be represented. Words and writing are not allowed in this exercise, only drawing.

3. Once each group has finished its drawing, each is displayed for the whole group. For each drawing, ask the others who did not draw that particular picture what they see in the picture, and list these qualities and attributes on a piece of chart paper. As each drawing is considered in turn, a full list of descriptions is compiled.

Variations, Adaptations, and Developments

Once the lists of qualities have been created, they can be used to identify whether there are skills needed that are not currently in the group or to create messages for those who have these jobs or roles.

Why We Like It

This is a flexible exercise that can be used for a variety of purposes; it encourages reflection on the key attributes of particular groups of people.

When You Can Use It

- If a group is about to take on a new role or task (a research project, for example), this activity can be used to see what skills and attributes are needed.

- This activity can be used if a group wants to give a message to another group.

Issues to Consider

Facilitators should assure participants that artistic ability is unimportant and provide enough assurance to encourage participants to draw.

Materials

Chart paper, pens in lots of colors, and imagination!

Activity Force Field Analysis

Purpose

- To explore the following questions:
  - What will help us achieve our goal?
  - What will work against us?
  - How can we maximize the strengths and diminish the weaknesses of our plan?

How We Do It

1. It is important that participants be in groups with others whom they are actually going to be working with. Ideally, groups should contain four to six people, but you may need to be flexible about this. Give each small group a piece of flipchart paper and some pens. Demonstrate the activity to the whole group. First, draw a circle in the middle of the paper, then two horizontal lines extending from the circle to the paper's edges, dividing the paper in half.

HELPING FACTORS

GOAL

HINDERING FACTORS

2. Have each group write their most immediate goal in the circle on their paper. On separate pieces of paper, the members then make two lists: a list of things that will help them achieve their goal and a list of things that will hinder them in reaching their goal. Once the lists are complete, they transfer the lists onto the flipchart. They must judge the strength and importance of the items on their lists. The things that will help most go on the top half of the paper, near the goal. The things that will most hinder go on the bottom half of the paper, near the goal. Less important factors are placed a little farther away from the goal. Relatively unimportant or weak factors are placed far from the goal.

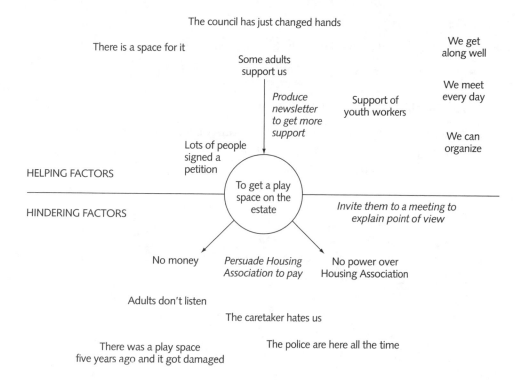

The council has just changed hands

There is a space for it

We get along well

Some adults support us

We meet every day

Produce newsletter to get more support

Support of youth workers

We can organize

Lots of people signed a petition

HELPING FACTORS

To get a play space on the estate

HINDERING FACTORS

Invite them to a meeting to explain point of view

No money

Persuade Housing Association to pay

No power over Housing Association

Adults don't listen

The caretaker hates us

There was a play space five years ago and it got damaged

The police are here all the time

3. Ask the group members to devise a series of actions that will do two things: move the positive factors that are farther away from the goal nearer to it (strengthen their effect) and move the hindering factors as far away from the goal as possible (weaken their effect). The group members write these actions on the flipchart paper.

Variations, Adaptations, and Developments

This activity can also be performed to create a visual representation of a SWOT analysis, with the strengths and opportunities placed on the top half of the paper in order of importance and the weaknesses and threats on the bottom half.

Why We Like It

This activity allows participants to examine their strategy, in order to take full advantage of its strengths and lessen its weaknesses. It offers a simple, clear visual illustration of what is on their side, what is against them, and a way forward. It assists in the preparation of the action plan.

When You Can Use It

This activity is one of a series used in the planning process, at the end of the "how" stage.

Issues to Consider

Sometimes the factors working against the group outnumber those that will help. This is not necessarily a problem, but it may cause the group to look again at whether the goal they have set for themselves is realistic.

Materials

Flipchart paper and markers. Small sticky notes are also useful; items can be written on them and moved around on the paper during the process of reaching agreement on where they should be placed.

Worst Nightmare

Purpose

- To help group members get advice on concerns they have about doing something new

- To address group members' fears about doing something new

How We Do It

1. Ask people, working alone, to think of their worst nightmare or greatest worry about a new thing they are considering doing.

2. Form small groups. (It is best to have a total of four or five groups.) Give each group a flipchart page, then have them draw a box in the center of the page and divide the paper into four parts. Have participants share their nightmares. The group should then choose one nightmare and write it inside the box. That group then passes the paper to the next group.

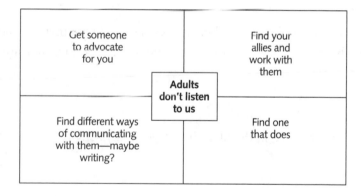

3. The chart paper is passed from group to group, so that each group's nightmare can be considered by the other groups, who each make a suggestion about addressing the worry. One suggestion is written in each part of the divided paper. At the end, the paper is returned to the original group. They consider the suggestions and decide on something they will actually do to reduce this concern.

Variations, Adaptations, and Developments

- You can suggest that the participants leave one extra box in which the original group can write their decision about what they are going to do in light of the advice and suggestions they have been given.

- Ideas can be written on sticky notes and arranged according to the group's likes and dislikes.

- Once all the sheets are completed and each nightmare has been offered a number of solutions, spread all the pieces of chart paper on the floor. Ask everyone in the large group to read them all and then

  - Mark ideas they think will work with a checkmark

  - Star ideas they most want to try

- Ask each group to develop their response to their own concern and prepare a presentation on how it could be implemented for the rest of the participants. That is, each group will answer the question "How can we overcome this nightmare?"

Why We Like It

This activity helps people see that there are ways to deal with their anxieties. It also shows them how their colleagues or fellow students can be an important source of support.

When You Can Use It

This exercise can be used in the planning stage of any activity.

Materials

Flipchart paper, pens of different colors, sticky notes (optional).

Activity Now/Soon/Later

Purpose

- To make a plan
- To decide who does what
- To decide on broad timing

How We Do It

1. Each group planning an action is invited to write down an action plan by using a matrix with nine cells. The time frame is indicated across the top, while the responsibility assignments run down the left side.

Time Frame			
Responsibility for Task	Now	Soon	Later
Us			
Us, with help			
Others			

2. Ask group members to list the activities necessary to carry out their ideas for action on a separate sheet or on sticky notes. Then ask them to answer the following questions:

   - Who will do it?
   - When does it have to happen?

3. Every activity should be written into one of the boxes. For example, a task to be done "now" by "us" goes in the upper-left cell; one to be done "soon" by "us, with help" goes in the center cell. When every activity has been allocated a time and a responsible person (or persons), then the action plan is complete.

Why We Like It

The plan is flexible; it commits people to a rough time frame rather than specific dates. It can be changed easily after the training. It admits the involvement of other parties but places the major responsibility on the participants themselves. It can be used by people of all ages and in any position. We have known people to take the chart back to the office with them and put it up on their wall to remind them of what needs to happen.

When You Can Use It

This type of plan is produced during the "act" phase of the Social Action process and used after the training session is over.

Issues to Consider

There should never be anything in the lower-left box, meaning that "others" are responsible for a task that must be done "now." Social Action begins with the people in the room. We cannot rely on outsiders to begin things for us.

Materials

As usual, flipchart paper and markers. Small sticky notes also work well because they can be moved from one place to another on the matrix.

Activity The Swimming Pool

Purpose

- To ask the following questions:
  - How confident do I (or we) feel?
  - Where am I in relation to other group members?

How We Do It

1. Draw a representation of a swimming pool containing as much detail as possible: a shallow end, a deep end, ladders leading to both, ladders in the middle, a high diving board, a medium-level board, a springboard, a changing room, a lifeguard, an entrance and exit, a spectators' gallery, and so on. Explain what you are drawing as it appears on the flipchart paper. Once the pool is complete, ask group members to take turns drawing themselves in the pool according to the terms you specify. You might instruct participants to use the pool to illustrate the stage they are at in their classroom practice, to show how confident they are as Social Action trainers, or to represent what stage the group is at right now.

2. Once everybody has placed themselves within the drawing, invite the participants to make observations about the completed picture. What do they notice? What does this say about the individuals or the group? Does anything require immediate attention?

Variations, Adaptations, and Developments

Group members often want to add their own detail to the pool and its environs; this should be encouraged. The group may discover another metaphor that they find more meaningful than a swimming pool, and the teacher-facilitator will need to judge whether the new suggestion is as rich.

Why We Like It

This activity provides group members with an extended metaphor through which they can discuss their feelings of comfort, confidence, uneasiness, fear, tiredness, and so on. The activity provides a less threatening way of bringing these matters to light than simply having a discussion.

When You Can Use It

This activity works best with a group of people who have been together for some time and feel it is time to take stock of how they are working together. It is also a suitable way to begin team-building sessions. It works for groups that are engaged in a new activity once they have embarked on a course of action. Through this activity, group members can consider how they feel at this point and what help is necessary for them to continue.

Issues to Consider

Sometimes group members hide behind the metaphor to avoid having a serious, honest discussion. The teacher-facilitator may occasionally need to remind group members that "this isn't really a swimming pool." Similarly, sometimes group members with a grievance use the exercise to hurl veiled abuse at colleagues. In these instances, the teacher-facilitator should accept that the metaphorical approach may not be helpful and open a more explicit conversation with the group.

Materials

Flipcharts, colored pens, a clean floor to sit on.

Activity **Messages**

Purpose

- To talk to the outside world
- To create a formula for campaigning
- To create momentum

How We Do It

1. Give the participants four prompts, and ask them to complete the sentences. The prompts are as follows:

   You must . . .

   Please remember . . .

   What about trying . . . ?

   It would be a good idea if . . .

   Ask the group to complete the sentences as messages to be delivered to policymakers, institutions, authorities, or managers that can have some effect on the group's goals.

2. Collect the messages, and have the group decide on a method of delivering them to the appropriate people. This can be done through an intermediary, by the participants themselves, by letter, or through a written summary or report on the course itself.

Why We Like It

The prompts are written in the form of a demand, a reminder, a challenge, and an inspiration. This makes participants think through what they wish to happen in a more complete way than if they were simply asked to produce recommendations. It also lends forward momentum to the work, taking it outside the training room or classroom.

When You Can Use It

This activity works best at the end of a stage of a project, when the participants have clarified some of their ideas and now want a response from the outside world.

Issues to Consider

Sometimes participants are uncomfortable making demands and may avoid doing this directly; however, if possible, they should be encouraged to find a way of wording a demand they are happy with.

REFERENCES

Betts, G. T., and Kercher, J. K. *Autonomous Learner Model.* Greely, Colo.: Autonomous Learning Publications & Specialists, 1999.

Centre for Social Action and the Guinness Trust. Youth*agenda: A Good Practice Guide to Working with Young People on Their Home Ground.* Leicester, U.K.: Centre for Social Action, 2000. [http://www.dmu.ac.uk/faculties/his/research/centreforsocialaction/index.jsp].

Critics of Society, Class of 2003, Sparks High School, Sparks, Nevada. "Changing Our World." *Inland: A Journal for Teachers of English Language Arts,* Fall–Winter, *25*(1), 11–12. (Published by the Idaho Council of Teachers of English and Inland Northwest Council of Teachers of English, Moscow, Idaho.)

Dewey, J. *The Child and the Curriculum and School and Society.* Chicago: University of Chicago Press, 1956.

Dynamix. *Participation—Spice It Up! Practical Tools for Engaging Children and Young People in Planning and Consultations.* Cardiff, U.K.: Save the Children, 2002.

Freire, P. *Pedagogy of the Oppressed.* Harmondsworth, U.K.: Penguin, 1970.

Hesse, H. *Siddhartha.* New York: Bantam Classics, 1982.

Holt, J. *The Underachieving School.* Harmondsworth, U.K.: Penguin, 1970.

Holt, J. *Instead of Education: Ways to Help People Do Things Better.* Harmondsworth, U.K.: Penguin, 1976.

Hope, A., and Timmel, S. *Training for Transformation: A Handbook for Community Workers.* Vol. 1. London: Intermediate Technology Publications, 1999.

Huitt, W. "Bloom et al.'s Taxonomy of the Cognitive Domain." [http://chiron.valdosta.edu/whuitt/col/cogsys/bloom.html]. 2000. Retrieved May 4, 2003.

Illich, I. *Deschooling Society.* Harmondsworth, U.K.: Penguin, 1970.

Illich, I. *After Deschooling, What?* London: Writers and Readers Publishing Cooperative, 1973.

Mullender, A., and Ward, D. *Self-Directed Groupwork: Users Take Action for Empowerment.* London: Whiting and Birch, 1991.

O'Brien, T. *The Things They Carried.* New York: Broadway Books, 1998.

Willinsky, J. *The New Literacy: Redefining Reading and Writing in the Schools.* New York: Routledge, 1990.

RESOURCES FOR FURTHER READING

About the NWP-CSA Collaboration

National Writing Project website: www.writingproject.org/r/socialaction

Activities and Resources

Badham, B. *Act by Right: Skills for the Active Involvement of Children and Young People in Making Change Happen.* Leicester, U.K.: National Youth Agency, 2004.

Benson, C., Christian, S., Gooch, W., and Goswami, D. *Writing to Make a Difference: Classroom Projects for Community Change.* New York: Teachers College Press, 2002.

Betts, G. T., and Kercher, J. K. *Autonomous Learner Model.* Greeley, Colo.: Autonomous Learning Publications & Specialists, 1999.

Centre for Social Action and the Guinness. Trust Youth*agenda: A Good Practice Guide to Working with Young People on Their Home Ground.* Leicester, U.K.: Centre for Social Action, 2000.

Dynamix. *Participation, Spice It Up: Practical Tools for Engaging Children and Young People in Planning and Consultations.* Cardiff, U.K.: Save the Children, 2002.

Hope, A., and Timmel, S. *Training for Transformation: A Handbook for Community Workers.* Vols. 1–4. London: Intermediate Technology Publications, 1999.

Sapin, K., and Watters, G. *Learning from Each Other: A Handbook for Participative Learning and Community Work Learning Programmes.* Manchester, U.K.: William Temple Foundation, 1990.

Ideas and Concepts

Freire, P. *Pedagogy of the Oppressed.* Harmondsworth, U.K.: Penguin, 1970.

Mullender, A., and Ward, D. *Self-Directed Groupwork: Users Take Action for Empowerment.* London: Whiting and Birch, 1991.

National Writing Project and Nagin, C. *Because Writing Matters: Improving Student Writing in Our Schools.* San Francisco: Jossey-Bass, 2003.

Smith, M. *Creators Not Consumers.* Leicester, U.K.: National Association of Youth Clubs Publications, 1982.

Willinsky, J. *The New Literacy: Redefining Reading and Writing in the Schools.* New York: Routledge, 1990.

Willow, C. *Participation in Practice: Children and Young People as Partners in Change.* London: Children's Society, 2002.

INDEX

C

Cary, C., 25

Centre for Social Action (CSA) [UK], 2–4, 31, 33, 43, 87

Changing Your Mind activity, 134–135

Chantel (student), 34, 38

Character education curriculum, 41

Chekana (student), 33, 37, 38

Chris (student), 38

Churchill, W., 33–34

Cierra (student), 37

Civil rights movement, 67–69

Class behavior: as classroom issue, 22; student empowerment evidenced by, 23–24

Classroom discussions: on dissatisfaction/truths about school programs, 20–21; on library checkout policies, 11–14; on playground problems and solutions, 14–17; using Social Action to facilitate, 20

Classroom promises (rules), 14

Classroom recommendations: on building community in Social Action work, 100–102; to facilitate Social Action process, 100; regarding accountability and support, 103–104; on setting for Social Action, 102–103; for Social Action facilitation, 97–98; on Social Action questions, 98–100; on successful Social Action projects, 104–105

Classrooms: facilitating democratic, 59–60; recommendations for the, 97–105; as safe environment, 97–98; Social Action redefinition of professionals in the, 92–94; as Social Action setting, 102–103; student behavior issue in, 22; student empowerment evidenced in, 23–24. *See also* Schools; Teacher-facilitators

Codes activity, 132–133

Community: identity, method, and purpose stages of building, 100–102; Social Action responsibilities by, 93*fig*; Youth Dreamers' collaboration with, 28–29

Community Action elective course, 25, 31–35. *See also* Youth Dreamers (Baltimore)

Community Vocabulary activity, 115–116

Creative Writing Workshop: facilitating democratic classroom in, 59–60; Movie Poster activity, 60; Sacred Writing activity of, 58–59; Social Action to restructure the, 57–59, 60–61; "Who Am I" poem activity, 60–61

Creech, S., 15

Crippen, S., 25

Critics of Society course: collaborative student article written on, 53–56; described, 51; introduction of Social Action to, 51–53. *See also* Sparks High School (Nevada)

CSA (Centre for Social Action) [UK], 2–4, 31, 33, 43, 87

Curriculum: Creative Writing Workshop, 57–61; Critics of Society, 52–56; literacy education, 1–4; Social Action applications to specific types of, 39–41, 84. *See also* Teaching

D

Davis, E. A., 67, 82, 83

DeKalb County landfill issues, 45–49

DeKalb County recycling issue, 47

DeKalb Neighborhoods Coalition, 48

Desegregation (school), 67–68

Devising the Vision activity, 102, 117–118

District of Columbia: barriers to civic engagement in, 71; John Philip Sousa Middle School of, 67–72; Shaw Junior High School, 70

exploring Social Action applications, 5–7, 35; interaction of Social Action with teaching practices by, 81–82; Social Action benefits for, 85–86. *See also* Students

Teaching: critical opportunities of teachable moments during, 82–83; interaction of Social Action process with, 81–82. *See also* Curriculum; Literacy education

Technology curriculum, 40–41

Tenaya (student), 47

Things They Carried, The (O'Brien), 53

Thoreau, H. D., 53

Three C's activity, 138–139

Tiffani (student), 36, 38

Towson University, 28

Treasure I See activity, 74–75

Turn the Corner Achievement Program, 38

U

Umoja (Unity) Circle [SWIS], 44

University of Maryland's Law Clinic, 28, 29

Uprisings (John Philip Sousa Middle School newspaper), 70

V

Villa Julie College, 28

W

Walker, L., 47

Washington, K., 70

Washington Post, 67–68

Website (Social Action), 43

"What" Social Action stage, 51–52, 68, 88, 90

"Who Am I" (poem), 60

"Why" Social Action stage, 52, 90–91

Willinsky, J., 1

Wilson, W., 69, 71

Worst Nightmare activity, 147–148

Writing Bible—Everything You Need to Know to Write Well (class handbook), 23

Y

Young-Smith, T., 25

Youth Dreamers (Baltimore): background information on, 25–26; becoming a nonprofit organization, 29; challenges of Social Action methods used by, 36–39; collaboration between community and, 28–29; Community Action course foundation of, 25, 31–35; dramatic success of, 3–4; fundraisers and presentations of, 27–28, 34–35; origins of, 26–27; reflections on process and successes of, 29–30, 35

Youth as Resources, 27, 28

Youth Venture, 28

Z

Zakiyah (student), 37, 38